SILK PAINTING

New ideas and textures

JILL KENNEDY AND
JANE VARRALL

Dover Publications, Inc., New York

First published in 1993 by B. T. Batsford Ltd., 4 Fitzhardinge St., London W1H 0AH England.

Library of Congress Cataloging-in-Publication Data

Kennedy, Jill.
    Silk painting : new ideas and textures / Jill Kennedy and Jane Varrall.
        p.   cm.
    Originally published: London : B.T. Batsford, 1993.
    Includes index.
    ISBN 0-486-27909-X
    1. Silk painting. I. Varrall, Jane. II. Title.
TT851.K46 1994
746.6—dc20
                                  93-6115
                                  CIP

Cover illustration
Permanent marker pens on pongée 9

ACKNOWLEDGEMENTS

We would like to thank our husbands and our families for their continued support and encouragement. We would also like to thank Sarah for reading, Moriko for drawing and Christine for typing.

Photographs taken by:
J.P. Van Den Wayenberg
Fotostudio Jean-Pierre
Mechelsesteenweg 232
3060 Sterrebeek
Belgium

CONTENTS

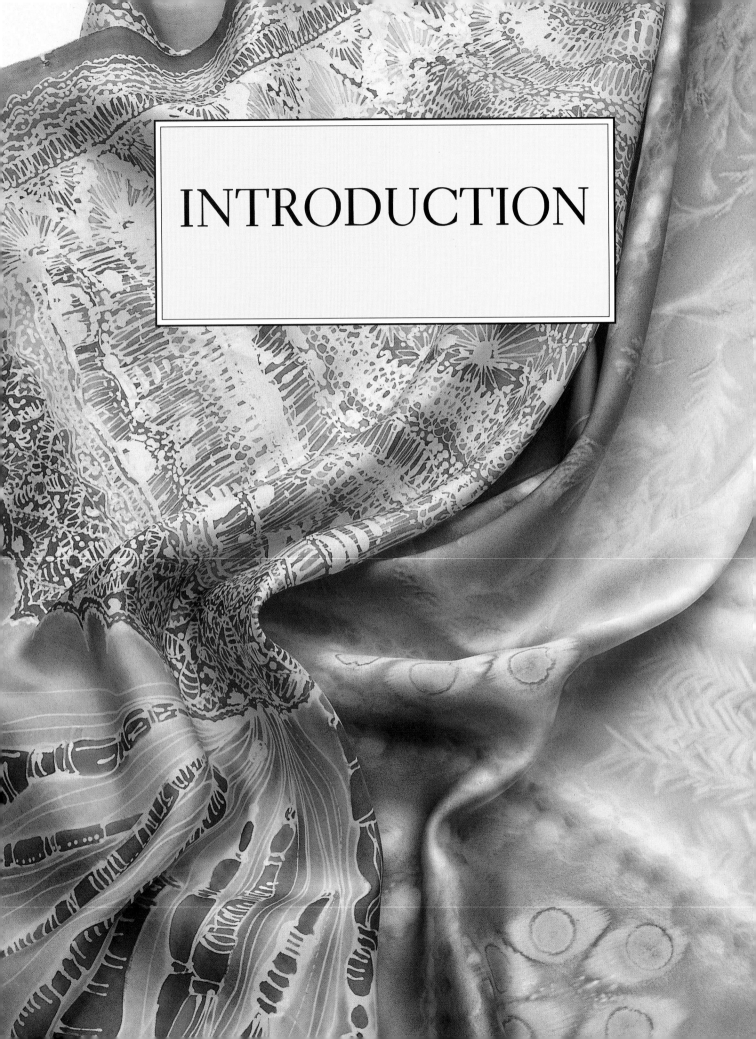

INTRODUCTION

One of the most exciting aspects of silk painting must be the opportunity that it provides for creating striking, subtle, vivid or even extraordinary 'textures' of colour. In this book we show you how to create these textures, using a wide range of equipment and techniques. We have ourselves enjoyed experimenting with different dyes, silks and substances, and here pass on to you practical instructions and advice based on our experience. Our own results provide the illustrations for the book.

You too can paint, print, spray, stencil, spatter, sprinkle, smear, blow, draw and dribble on silk! We will show you how to sponge, pleat, crackle, comb and crumple. Some of the techniques do not demand tremendous artistic ability – just enthusiasm and a willingness to experiment. Never be afraid to try new ideas, and to invent your very own technique: you will almost certainly be pleased with the results, and you will have the satisfaction of knowing that your work is entirely original.

We have based the book on twelve different techniques for creating 'texture' on silk. These include the use of dyes, wax, gutta, anti-spread, sugar, salt, alcohol, thickener, pens and even the sun. Each chapter covers one of the techniques, and shows you the various effects that can be obtained from its use. The specific materials that you will require are discussed, and clear instructions are given on how to use them.

At the end of the book you will find a section on materials, equipment and fixing, describing all the dyes, silk and equipment needed, and also giving hints about the workplace and how to fix, wash and care for your silk. Lastly, we have provided a comprehensive list of manufacturers and stockists so that you will have no trouble in purchasing your silk-painting equipment. We have also listed services which provide steam-fixing, hand rolling of scarves, or the making up of your silk into items such as ties, waistcoats or bags.

We have really enjoyed using these techniques, and hope that this book will enable you – whether you are an amateur or a professional silk painter – to enjoy them too.

Textures in pastel.
(Left) Wax
(Right) Helio

-1-

WATER

Watercolour is an exciting medium to use on silk, as it allows a very free approach. This technique involves painting directly on to the stretched silk, using ordinary tap water and dyes.

Blending, merging, flowing; spraying, splashing, spattering; daubing, dribbling and dripping: the dyes just flow on the silk, and you do not have complete control. You must decide just how much dye to put on your brush, and, after several attempts, you will learn how far the dyes will flow. It is a rather unpredictable technique in that you cannot always guarantee which way the dye will run, and so the picture you had in mind may not quite resemble the finished work. Often, however, the end results are even more dramatic and exciting than you had envisaged, and they are certainly always unique. The dye will run as far as it can when there is no barrier of gutta or wax, and no anti-spread coating on the silk. Interesting textures may also be obtained by what is sometimes known as washing out, in which the painted silk is rubbed with various applicators to remove the dye.

Have fun experimenting with this technique, and enjoy the freedom that it brings.

(Previous page)
Abstract waterfall on crêpe de Chine

EQUIPMENT NEEDED

- Silk
- Water
- Frame and pins
- Masking tape
- Dyes
- Diluent
- Brushes, applicators, palettes, jars
- Cotton wool

Different brands of dye and weights of silk react very differently with this technique.

SILK

Watercolour reacts very differently on the various silks. When a finer silk such as pongée 5 is used, the dyes spread across the fibres very quickly and merge into each other. As you can see in the photograph opposite, the flower is not really distinguishable in the pongée 5 sample on the left. An entirely different effect can be created by using a thicker silk, such as a pongée 10 or a thick crêpe de Chine. The dye will still retain a soft outline on this silk, but will not spread as far, so that greater definition can be achieved.

DYES

Silk-painting dyes really lend themselves to the watercolour technique, as they run so well into each other and merge beautifully when wet. The brand of dye used also has a great effect on the end result. The thinner, transparent, steam-fixed dyes flow very easily across the silk, sometimes covering too large an area, especially if you have overloaded your brush or applicator.

The thicker, iron-on dyes do not spread quite as easily. If you are more restrained and like to have greater control over your work, therefore, it would be advisable for you to use the iron-fixed dyes on a thick crêpe de Chine. If you are using the washing-out technique, the steam-fixed dyes work best.

WET SILK

You can gain greater control over the dye by painting the stretched silk beforehand with clean water or diluent (see overleaf). If you then paint your design while the silk is still damp (but not too wet) the dye will not travel as far. The pigments in the dye sometimes separate when painted on to wet silk, as can be seen on the green leaves in the right-hand sample on the opposite page.

LARGE BACKGROUND AREAS

Backgrounds or large areas can be extremely difficult to paint evenly. The dye should be applied to large areas using a large brush, cotton pad or foam applicator.

Always make sure that enough dye has been prepared to cover the whole area, as it is very difficult to obtain the exact shade if you have mixed a wonderful original colour. Any unused dye may be stored for future use in an airtight container.

Flower shapes painted on (from left to right) pongée 5, crêpe de Chine and pongée 10 with a wet background

The dye should be painted quickly and evenly across the silk from side to side, working down the fabric. When the brush needs re-filling with dye, always re-join at the edge, never in the middle, to avoid a build-up of dye in one area. If you are working on an extremely large area, it may help to get another person to work with you, and the entire piece of silk should be sprayed or painted with water beforehand. The damp surface helps the dye to spread and avoids any hard edges.

The silk should be very tightly stretched on the frame. Once it has been painted or sprayed with water it may need re-stretching, as it tends to stretch and sag.

DILUENT

Instead of using water alone to wet the silk and help the dyes to spread evenly, you can use a special liquid called diluent (also known as diffusant, diffusion fondnet, anticerne, diluant and dilutant). Diluent aids the uniform spreading and merging of the dye, thus avoiding hard lines and watermarks. It can be purchased in a concentrated form or ready-mixed, so make sure that you read the label for instructions on how to prepare it for use.

Diluent may be mixed in large quantities and stored ready for use in a large plastic bottle. The silk can be covered with diluent instead of water and then painted with dye while damp, or the dye can be mixed with diluent and painted on to the dry silk. Some silk painters use diluent in preference to water with all their dyes for mixing, as it does promote even colouration. This is really an added expense that you can do without, as most of the time water is quite adequate.

GRADED WASH

Simple but very effective wash effects can be painted by simply blending different colours or tones of one colour into each other. The background can be dampened first, as this will promote even blending. When shading in this way it is necessary to work quickly, before the dyes have time to dry. Have all your equipment and dyes organized, as speed is essential.

Load a large, soft brush, sponge applicator or cotton wool with full-strength dye and paint across the top of the silk, taking care not to lift the brush until you reach the end of the silk. Working quickly, add a little water to the dye and lay down a second stripe of colour directly beneath the first, and overlapping it slightly. Repeat this process. Keep adding water to the dye with each successive stripe, and make sure that the stripes of dye blend into each other. If you have made a marked dark line by mistake, try rubbing it with damp cotton wool.

BLENDING COLOURS

Blending colours into one another is very effective, as the colours merge to create a soft, subtle effect. The silk can be dampened with water or diluent before you stretch it into the frame, or, alternatively, sprayed or painted with water or diluent after it has been stretched.

Paint an area of colour with soft, fluid waves as shown opposite, and then, before it dries, paint another colour right next to it and overlapping slightly. Let the colours merge into each other. Continue to paint the waves on to the silk, using three or four colours or indeed as many as you wish. Every time you introduce a new colour, make sure that each area of dye overlaps slightly on to the next colour. Rub firmly with your brush or cotton wool to ensure that the colours merge into each other. Do not be frightened to rub hard; the silk is very strong and will not rub away as paper would do.

MOTTLED COLOURS

A mottled effect is easily achieved with the watercolour technique, and is useful for clouds and backgrounds. Wet the silk and, while it is still wet (as opposed to just damp), roll a large, dye-filled brush around in different directions. Add more water if necessary, and more colours if you wish. Again, if hard lines and marks appear, try rubbing with cotton wool and water.

There are endless ways of achieving different effects using water. Ten samples follow (see overleaf for illustrations).

Water lines on a dry background

Paint the entire piece of silk green, and wait for it to dry completely. Using water *only*, paint the wavy lines. The pigments in the dye will move to the edges of the water leaving dark edges – so simple to achieve and yet so effective. You could be forgiven for thinking that someone had spent hours drawing the jagged-edged dark lines.

Graded wash and blended colours

Be sure to use clean water for the best results. Keep two containers of water at hand: one to clean your brush, and one which will remain clean for achieving all the effects. A hairdryer can sometimes be used to stop the creeping of the dye when a good effect has already been achieved. This washing-out technique works very well with steam-fixed dyes.

Drops of dye on a dry background

Paint the background and allow it to dry. Drop on spots of green and pink dye and leave to dry. Paint more spots inside these spots. The water

11

will loosen the dye and cause it to flow, while the dark pigments will gather together in an irregular, jagged, hard-edged line.

Spray on a dry background

Paint the background green and allow to dry completely. Spray water using an old spray bottle or atomizer and allow to dry. Spray again and leave to dry. Repeat the spraying-and-drying process until you have created an interesting mottled effect.

Lines on a dry background

Paint the background pale pink and leave to dry. Paint a series of stripes – which do not touch each other – in one colour. Leave to dry before painting more stripes. Repeat this process, making sure that each set of stripes is dry before applying more dye.

Stripes painted on direct

Do not wet or paint the background. Paint a series of stripes, slightly overlapping them so that they merge together.

Different textures.
Top row, from left to right:
    water lines on a dry background
    drops of dye on a dry background
    spray on a dry background
    lines on a dry background
    stripes painted on direct
Bottom row, from left to right:
    over-painting in detail
    stripes painted on a wet background
    water on a dry, painted background
    wet drops on a wet background
    wet lines on a wet background

Over-painting in detail

Paint the background pale pink and, while still damp, add green and pink stripes. Allow to dry. Add the detail using a fine sable or small silk-painting brush: pick up a small amount of dye and stroke any excess off on a rag (the less dye on the brush, the more fine detail can be obtained). The more coats or layers of dye the silk has had, the easier it will be to paint on fine details. This works well with iron-on dyes, as they do not spread as easily.

Stripes painted on a wet background

Wet the background and, while still damp, paint stripes of colour. Leave to dry naturally; the colours will merge beautifully with long, finger-like projections similar to stalagmites or stalactites.

Water on a dry, painted background

Paint the background with a mottled pink, maroon, green and brown wash. Leave to dry. Paint on water in uneven lines and blobs.

Wet drops on a wet background

Paint the background green and, while damp, drop water on to the silk. The pigments will group around the edge of the drop of water, forming soft, flower-like shapes.

Wet lines on a wet background

Paint the background maroon, and, while still damp, paint on lines of clean water. The pigments will be pushed sideways to form darker, soft lines.

Wet-on-wet flowers (*see below*)

Paint the stretched silk with water and blot off any excess, so that the silk is damp rather than wet. Speed is essential with this technique, as hard lines will appear if the silk is too dry. Paint the flowers and leaves as quickly as possible so that they merge together while still wet. It is useful to use diluent if you are painting a large area, as the diluent takes longer to dry, giving you more time to paint the picture. Details can then be added. The difficulty is knowing when to stop: if hard-edged lines and watermarks start to appear

and you wanted a soft, fluid look, you are too late! You do not need to use many colours, as, where the dyes merge and blend, new colours are automatically created.

Wet-on-dry tartan (*see opposite*)

Paint the stretched silk with dye and let it dry. A graded wash from dark pink to green was used here. A hairdryer can be used to speed up the drying process, but be careful: if you hold the nozzle too near the silk and one area dries too quickly, a watermark may appear.

Using greens and deep pinks, paint vertical lines and let them dry naturally (using a hairdryer at this point would speed up the process too much and not give the pigments in the dye time to move). Be careful not to overload the brush with dye, as this will result in uneven lines and

Wet-on-wet flowers

blobs. When painting the stripes, try to get from one side to the other without lifting the brush. If you do run out of paint in the middle of a stripe, start at the other end and work across to ensure that the stripe is as even as possible. Wait until you see how far the dye is spreading before starting the next stripe, or the stripes may blur into each other.

When the first set of stripes is dry, repeat this process in the opposite direction to create the tartan effect. Where the two lines of dye cross each other, a third hue is produced. This is a very easy technique, which works well with transparent dyes. Try experimenting with different colour combinations. Try the same process, but on a wet background. Try painting a wet tartan background and then, when it is dry, paint a finer lined tartan over this.

The large, abstract waterfall painting on pages 6–7 was painted on crêpe de Chine, using some of the techniques discussed in this chapter. Using dark and olive green and maroon dyes, wet the stretched silk and paint the background, working quickly to ensure that the silk is wet so that the colours are able to blend and merge. Allow to dry thoroughly. Now the fun really begins! Paint, daub, dribble and drop the water and dyes on to the soft background, stopping the flow of the dye when interesting shapes or edges are formed. Over-paint with more colours to draw out the shapes.

FIXING

With all the watercolour techniques discussed in this chapter, the dye needs to be fixed permanently into the silk. The method for doing this varies according to the dyes used. Check the instructions on your dye bottle in each case and see also pages 118–21.

Wet-on-dry tartan

TIPS

- Paint the silk with diluent or water first.
- Make sure that the silk is tightly stretched on the frame.
- Do not be frightened to rub silk firmly to blend dyes.
- Check that your brush is clean, especially before painting with water and pale colours.
- Make sure that you have enough dye colour prepared for watercolour washes. Remember that, the thicker the silk, the more dye is absorbed.

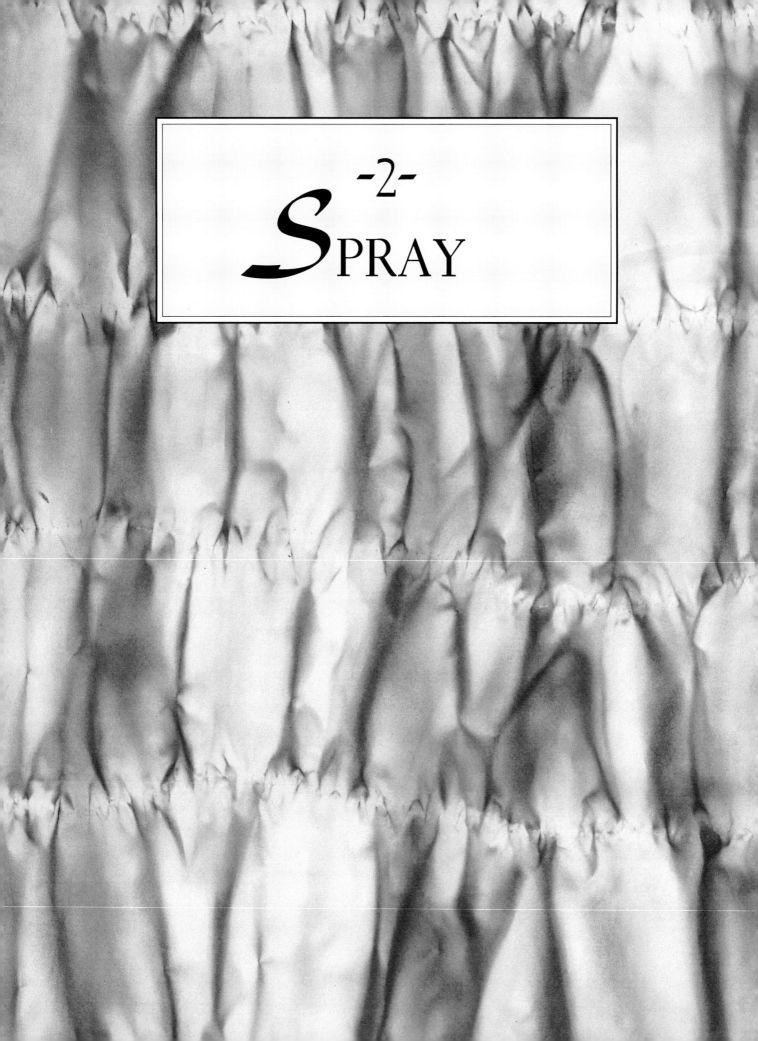

-2-
SPRAY

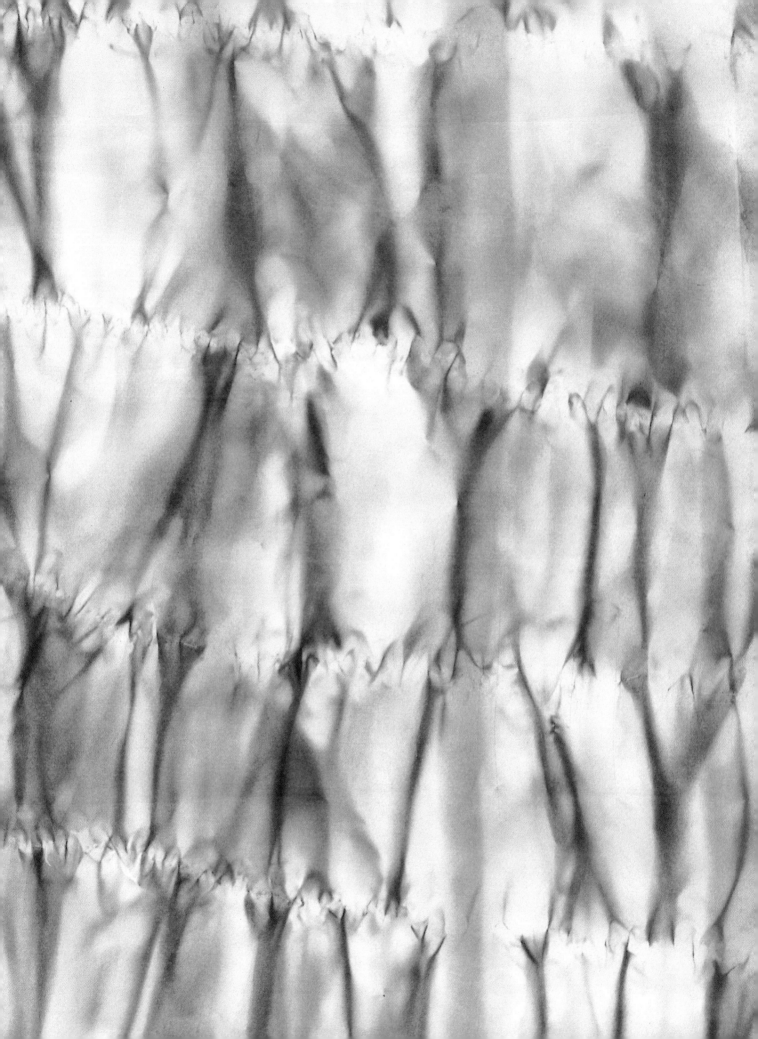

A very different texture can be achieved by using spray equipment on the silk. Fine layers of colour can be built up with tiny dots of dye, with the finished effect depending on the fineness of the nozzle used to spray.

To a certain extent, the quality of the spraying is not as effective on silk as on a paper surface because of the porous nature of the fabric. This can be altered a little by coating the surface with anti-spread (antifusant). This will be discussed in more detail on pages 72–81.

Masking the silk with a template in the form of a stencil, through which the dye is sprayed, creates a variety of patterns. Some of the images can be very detailed, or they can simply be used as background textures. Many other fabrics and forms can be used as the masking medium instead of a stencil, such as lace, leaves, grills, masking fluid and film.

Spraying is a skill which takes time to develop if very detailed shaded work is to be produced. Large background areas may be worked quite easily, however, if only mottled colour is needed.

(Previous page)
Ruched and sprayed crêpe de Chine

Equipment used for spraying.
From left to right:
    garden spray bottle
    mouth diffuser
    car spray paint
    Eco-spray and spray gun
    airbrush

EQUIPMENT NEEDED

The spraying equipment that you use will depend on the desired results, and on the expense that you can afford. You will need the following:

- Silk
- Water
- Eco-spray and compressed-air canister
- Diffuser or fixative sprayer
- Air pump
- Garden spray bottle
- Empty cleaning-product spray bottle
- Perfume atomizer
- Toothbrush, nailbrush, stiff brush
- Masking fluid
- Spray paint
- Anti-spread
- Stencilling equipment
- Airbrush and compressor
- Airgun and compressed-air canister
- Frame and pins
- Masking tape
- Dyes
- Diluent (see page 10)
- Brushes, applicators, palettes, jars
- Cotton wool
- Hairdryer
- Oiled card, acetate, card, masking film or polyphane
- Cutting board
- Craft knife
- Varnish
- Metal ruler
- Tracing paper

PREPARATION

Organizing the spraying area is very important. The fine spray-mist of dye can cover any surface, so make sure that you have plenty of polythene and newspaper to spread around. A dry, windless day is ideal for spraying out-of-doors and this is certainly preferable if you are using compressed-air canisters, as the gases in these are quite strong. Indoors it is always advisable to use a small face mask to protect your nose and mouth, as inhaling the dye particles in a confined space is inevitable.

It is useful to prop up your frame with the stretched silk against a wall

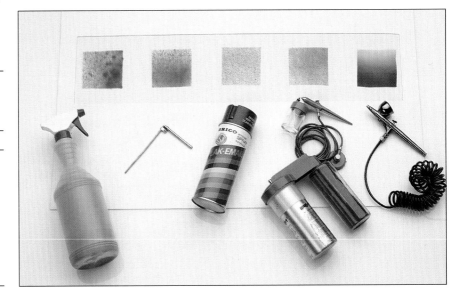

or garage door. Using large sheets of cardboard, try to construct a spray 'booth' to confine the mess of spraying. Remember to cover behind this area, as well as the floor.

SILK

Most types of silk can be used for the spraying technique, although dyes are absorbed very quickly on a finer weight. Spray very lightly and allow the silk to dry thoroughly between each coat. If you do not do so, the dye will saturate the silk and run down the fabric, or the colour will merge and the sprayed effect will be lost.

DYES

All silk-painting dyes can be used for this technique. Many special dyes for spraying on fabric are now readily available, and these dry quickly on the fabric. Do not use thicker dyes with the airbrush as it will be extremely difficult to clean. You will need to experiment with dyes, as you will find that the depth of colour alters when the dye is sprayed. The colour is much lighter after spraying than one would have expected, and therefore it will need to be mixed several shades darker. The application of a layer of anti-spread (antifusant) on to the surface will also alter the final sprayed colour; this can only really be seen after the silk has been fixed. If the depth of colour is very important, a test piece will need to be sprayed and fixed.

Car spray paint gives excellent results, as it dries very quickly after each application and allows fine layers of colour to be built up. The

Simple sprayed effects.
(Left) Crumpling
(Centre, top) Cross-pleating
(Centre, bottom) Pleating
(Right) Draping

main disadvantage is that the spray stiffens the fabric, so that the silk loses its malleable quality.

SIMPLE SPRAYED EFFECTS

The following experiments may be carried out using an Eco-spray, or an airgun and gas canister. These give a broad spraying jet. You must coat the surface of the silk with anti-spread beforehand. Each layer of dye must only be sprayed after the others have dried thoroughly.

Crumpling

A three-dimensional marbled effect is made by slightly dampening the silk and crunching it into a ball. Spray the paint from one side.

Re-arrange the creased ball and spray from the other side. For the final colour, re-arrange the ball once more and spray from a different angle. Use a hairdryer to speed up drying between layers.

Pleating

The pleated sample above shows the silk with random stripes at varying angles. The spray is directed from different sides of the fold each time, and the resulting colours are varied in weight and texture, giving a lovely, soft, striped effect. The folds are kept in place on the frame using three pronged pins. At each colour change, remove the pins and slightly alter the folds. If you want a uniform stripe, more care in the pleating and placing of the pins and more accurate measuring will also be necessary.

Cross-pleating

A tartan-plaid effect is created by using the same pleating, pinning and spraying technique as described for pleating. The silk is removed when dry, before being re-pinned and sprayed with the folds in the opposite direction. Compare this sample with that of the tartan watercolour on page 15 and you will see that spraying produces a much softer effect. The bands can be made broader and the stripes more uniform if wished. This is a very quick way of covering a piece of silk with colour.

Draping

Pin the silk loosely on to the frame, creating attractive folds in the fabric. Spray lightly from different angles to create three-dimensional draped effects. When dry, un-pin the silk and re-pin to create new folds. Spray on a second colour. This method makes an ideal background texture on a crêpe-de-Chine scarf.

Gathering

Using a fine thread, loosely gather the silk by hand in broad bands. Draw up into folds and place on a flat surface. Lightly spray over the gathers from two directions. Allow the silk to dry, then remove the running stitches and iron the silk flat. This method creates an unusual textured effect. Additional gathers could be sewn and a second colour sprayed.

A delicate, misty effect produced by over-spraying an attractive leaf shape, using two colours of car spray paint

SPRAYING OVER SHAPES WHICH RESIST

A very effective way of making patterns is to spray over solid shapes, and then to re-position them and spray again. The shapes may be moved and placed in a formal design, or attached on the silk at random. It will be difficult to spray with the frame in an upright position unless the shapes are secured on to the silk in some way, so either pin or lightly spraymount them. If the shapes are cut out of polyphane or masking film they will be sticky already and can simply be pressed gently on to the silk. Remember to draw the shapes on to the paper backing in reverse so that, when positioned, the design is the right way round.

Misty leaf design (*see below*)

Pin the leaf shapes on to the silk and spray lightly with pink car spray paint. Re-position the shapes several times and spray with green car spray paint until a soft overall pattern is created. The silk will be hard to the touch when dry. The paints do not need fixing into the silk.

Field of cow parsley (*see opposite*)

Cover the whole piece of stretched silk with anti-spread. Paint the delicate heads and stalks of the cow parsley with artist's masking fluid and a fine brush; this white gum will dry to form a barrier. Lightly spray the silk with blue dye near the heads, and green near the stalks and leaves. Dry the silk, then gently rub

Masking-tape stripes on fine pongée, using masking tape for the resist

away the fluid using your fingers. The masked line will remain bright white, having resisted the spray. Gutta or wax can be used as alternative resists; dry cleaning or white spirit will remove them afterwards.

Masking-tape stripes *(see right)*

Stretch the silk tightly on to the frame and press strips of masking tape firmly on to the surface. Place additional strips on top of each colour spray (these will resist the dye). Dry the silk and strips thoroughly, and then remove the masking tape to reveal the colourful stripes.

SPRAYING THROUGH SHAPES

This technique is great fun because the objects through which you spray will give unexpected and unusual results. Household objects such as graters, grills and strainers can be used, and fabrics with an open weave or the open designs of lace are ideal.

The traditional method is to cut stencils and to spray through the shapes to form a pattern. This is a very quick way of covering silk with a design once the stencil has been prepared.

Formal stencil pattern *(see left)*

Rather formal, but still showing the interesting texture of spraying, this traditional design is cut out of flexible acetate. Coat the silk with anti-spread. Apply the dye colours using a mouth diffuser; you can see that the texture is much rougher than with the airbrush or airgun. A toothbrush can also be used to create this spattered effect. The stencil is laid on to the surface, allowing some dye to pass under the acetate; this has the effect of softening the design. If a crisp finish is required, the edges should be spraymounted on to the silk.

Spraying through shapes.
(Top) Formal stencil pattern
(Bottom left) Lace oddments
(Bottom right) Grater

Lace oddments (*see previous page*)

This subtle work is created by painting the background of the silk in a green wash of dye and drying it. Cover the surface of the silk with anti-spread, then place the prettily shaped lace oddments on to the silk and pin in position. Areas which remain without lace must be masked with newspaper to prevent them being covered with dye. Spray the lace again and again using shades of blue and maroon. The effect is quite mysterious and subtle.

Grater (*see previous page*)

Wash the background of the silk with pale green dye before coating with anti-spread. Place the hard grater on the surface of the silk and spray with maroon and navy dyes. Re-position the grater each time, before spraying through and around the shape. The contrast between the hard edges and soft background creates a dramatic effect.

MAKING A STENCIL

Most stencil-making equipment is now stocked in good art and craft shops. Traditional oiled card can be used, although clear acetate is better for matching up designs. A sharp-pointed cutting blade is essential for cutting the stencil, as is a cutting mat or wooden board. A metal ruler is useful for cutting against for straight edges, as a wooden ruler splinters easily.

Landscape at sunset. Torn-paper masking and the sprayed-through technique

1. Trace your design on to the stencil card using a black marker pen.
2. Place the cutting mat or board underneath the card and tape it firmly into place.
3. Hold the card firmly with one hand. Begin to cut the stencil, away from your fingers, with a pointed blade. Keep the blade upright and try to cut smoothly. Un-tape the stencil to cut around curves; turn the card slowly as you cut the shapes.
4. Prepare a flat surface for stencilling and cover it with clean paper. Stretch and tape the silk on to the paper. Alternatively, stretch the silk on to a frame and place this over a thick, even wad of paper.
5. Spraymount the stencil on to the stretched silk, or cut the stencil out of polyphane (which is already sticky). Another method of attaching is to use masking tape, although the dye could creep underneath this.
6. Spray through the stencil lightly and evenly. Dry the silk if possible before moving the stencil.

COMBINING THE METHODS OF SPRAYING

Your sprayed pictures can combine a mixture of processes. It will be necessary to plan the stages of your work carefully so that you can mask out areas that should not be sprayed.

Landscape at sunset (*see below*)

An Eco-spray or a mouth diffuser can be used for this work. Note how much more varied the texture of the spraying is here in comparison with *Planets* (opposite), where a finer spray has been achieved.

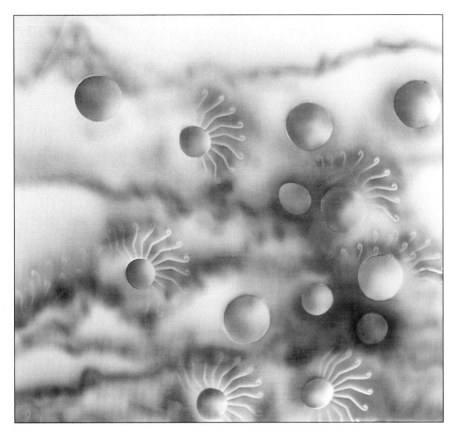

Planets. Masking film and airbrush technique

lifting away as you spray. All three colours – maroon, green and blue – are sprayed over and into the circles.

3. Try to create a three-dimensional effect with the planets by spraying heavily towards the top and left-hand side. Take care not to spray over the outer edge of the square of polyphane, or you will leave a hard edge.

4. The 'tendrils' from the planets are created by spraying over a thick wire shape. The spray is allowed to form hard edges. Some of these were softened afterwards by re-spraying.

5. The colours were used in their concentrated form, but note how pale they become when sprayed.

1. Tear a card outline for the mountains and place the template approximately in the centre.

2. Spray the graduated blue of the sky on and above the mountain shapes.

3. Lower the mountain outline on to the silk and spray with pink dye, slightly overlapping the blue.

4. Invert the mountain shape and cover up the pink layer with extra card. Spray below in pale blue to form the reflection.

5. Lower the mountain shape one more time and spray in pale green for the bottom foreground colour.

6. Finally, cut out a circle from a square of paper and place it in position on the sky. Spray through the hole with a deeper shade of pink to make the shape of the setting sun.

Planets (*see above*)

The final sample shows use of the airbrush. Although expensive, this can be very useful for silk painting, as the fine, adjustable spray produces delicate yet extremely effective shading. The dyes must be thin: steam-fixed dyes are ideal. Other dyes must be watered down unless designed for airbrushing.

1. Cut out two different-sized circles in polyphane. You will need at least two of both sizes, as well as the outer template of the circle (you will be spraying both *over* the circle and *into* the circle).

2. Place the circles at random on the silk (crêpe de Chine was used for this piece). The circles will stick to the surface when the paper backing is removed, which will stop them

TIPS

● Do not use too much spray-mount on the templates, or it will mark the silk.

● Make sure when applying the anti-spread liquid prior to spraying that you do not omit any area, or the dye will react differently on that spot.

● When stencilling, make sure that the underside of the stencil is clean before replacing on the silk. Otherwise, if you need to make an adjustment, you may have already marked the silk with dye.

● Do not hold the spray too near the silk. You may over-spray and saturate the fabric, causing runs.

-3-
SALT

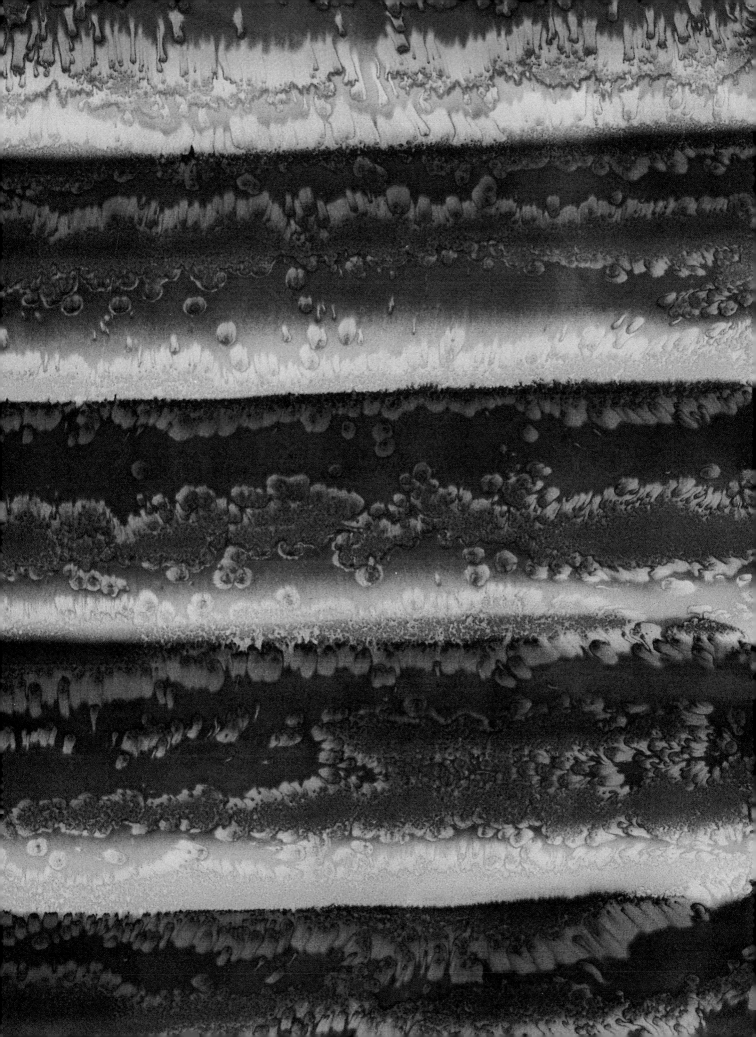

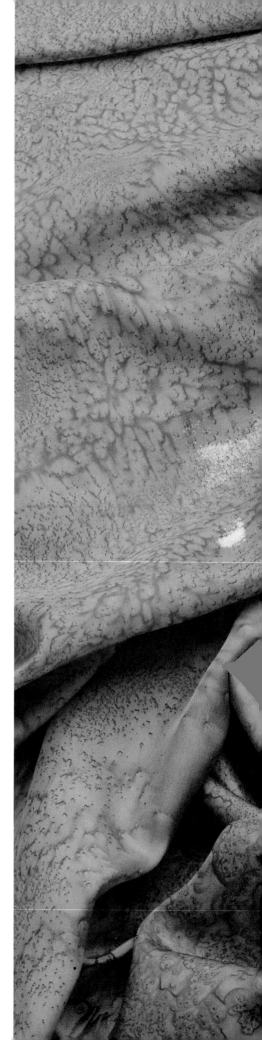

The salt technique is probably the easiest of all. It involves painting the silk with your chosen colours, sprinkling salt on to the damp silk and simply waiting for it to dry. The grains of salt attract the dye and soak it up from the surrounding area. The colour begins to flow in different directions as the salt picks up the dye, creating marvellous textures. This technique is so simple, and yet such stunning results can be produced.

As with the watercolour technique, the end result when using salt in this way is often beyond your control. The interesting textures obtained can resemble starry skies, fireworks, snowflakes, starbursts, mountains, rock formations, landscapes and crystalline shapes. All this just from sprinkling salt on to damp silk! Children and non-artists especially love this technique, as such professional-looking results can be achieved. One thing is certain – you will never be able to produce two identical pieces of work, no matter how hard you try.

EQUIPMENT NEEDED

- Silk
- Water
- Salt
- Frame and pins
- Masking tape
- Dyes
- Brushes, droppers, palette, jars
- Cotton wool

(Previous page)
Use of rock salt on bands of dye *(see page 30)*

Different weights of silk, brands of dye and types of salt will all react differently with this technique.

TYPES OF SALT

Very different textures may be obtained depending on the type of salt used. Fine table salt, sea salt, pearl salt, rock salt and dishwasher salt are all readily available and will all work with this technique.

Fine-grain salt from your kitchen or salt cellar will produce very fine, feathery effects and small stars or flowers. Coarse sea or rock salt is the ideal choice for a more dramatic effect: this will create larger forms reminiscent of mountains, forests and craggy rocks. Pearl-salt grains, being uniform in size, will produce a more even, rounded design. Special salt for this technique can also be bought from some silk-painting manufacturers. This salt works well with iron-fixed dyes. For the best results make sure that the salt is very dry. You can put it on a radiator in a tin, or even warm it up in the oven.

When you have finished, it is possible to shake the salt into a jar and use it again. It may sometimes be a little discoloured, however, and if this is the case it is not always worth the risk or expense of ruining the next piece of silk.

Textures created with salt.
(Left) Table salt
(Right) Rock salt
(Centre) Graded wash

SILK

This technique works very well on pongée 5–10 and crêpe de Chine. The thicker slubbed silks, wild silk and bourette do not react as well. It is wise to experiment on a sample test piece before starting a large project.

DYES

Undiluted, pure dyes produce strong lines and shapes. A softer, more flowing effect can be created by diluting the dyes with water. All brands of dye work well with this technique; transparent steam-fixed dyes produce a more definite movement than the iron-fixed dyes, which create a softer texture.

Some colours work much better than others. The dye really moves on dark colours such as browns, greens and blues, but is less effective on oranges and yellows. For some reason it rarely works on black, especially when steam-fixed dyes are used. Mixed dyes and compound colours produce good results. Certain mixed dyes separate while they are drying, forming shades and tones of their base colours.

The process is less effective with very diluted colours. An example of this can be seen in the graded-wash salt sample on the previous page.

Be very careful not to get any grains of salt into the dye bottle, as they will ruin the dye.

THE SALT TECHNIQUE

Paint the background

Stretch the silk tightly on to the frame. The dye can then be painted straight on to the fabric. To allow yourself more time before the silk dries, however, it is often advisable to paint or spray the fabric with water or diluent first before applying the dyes. It is vital that the silk is *damp*: not too dry, and not too wet. If the silk is too dry, the effect will be lost and only a few round spots and small shapes will develop. If the silk is too wet, and it is saturated with pools of dye, the salt drowns – the salt will become overloaded with dye and will not work effectively.

A mottled effect can be created by using several colours intermingled; the salt will blend them together. The silk also can be painted in stripes, circles or flower-like shapes.

Make sure that your workroom is not too hot and avoid direct spotlights or sunlight when using this technique, or the silk will dry too rapidly, not giving the salt a chance to work.

Sprinkle the salt

Sprinkle the salt on to the damp silk. Be careful not to use too much salt, as this hinders movement. Several grains are more effective than a huge pile.

Stripes

One quick-and-easy idea is to paint the colours in stripes using a thick brush or foam applicator, placing rock or sea salt along the lines where the two colours meet. This technique is shown in the photograph on pages 26–7.

Salt grains being placed to form a flower, and finished samples

Large salt flower

salt absorb as much dye as they are able, and all the time the silk is drying, the design is forming. You will be able to watch the dye flow as the salt crystals work, leaving the colour pigments as dark lines. Under each grain of salt a darker area will appear.

The silk may take up to half an hour or more to dry (you can leave it overnight if you wish). However, if after several minutes you like the design and do not wish it to 'move' any further, quickly tip the salt off and dry the silk using a hairdryer to prevent further movement.

Try saving the salt after you have brushed it off and using it on another coloured wet piece of silk. It will leave some of the old colour on the new silk.

When the silk is completely dry, brush the salt from the surface with a fine, soft brush. Fine table salt may stick to the silk: either scratch off the grains or remove the work from the frame and rub the silk together. The silk should be entirely free from salt before being fixed.

MIXED TECHNIQUES

The salt technique may be combined successfully with other techniques such as gutta, wax, sugar and so on. Salt-textured backgrounds help to relieve large plain areas.

When a mixed technique is being painted, leave the salt part until last if possible. Paint the plain areas first and let them dry. If the salt technique is used at the beginning,

Circles

Individual circles or flowers can be produced by painting the background one colour and placing a circle of salt grains on to the dye. A drop of water or dye can be added to the middle of the flower. You can actually be more controlled, and place the salt grains by hand in an accurate circle, if you have the patience! Remember that the silk will dry if you take too long.

The salt can be placed on the dry silk first, before the dye and water are painted on. This way you have longer to arrange the salt crystals, but it is difficult not to disturb them when adding the dye. Always work on a flat surface, making sure that

the salt crystals do not move once applied. Leave the silk to dry.

The texture created with this technique is achieved through the interaction of the silk, dye, water and salt. The effect is different every time, depending on:

- the colour and intensity of the dye
- the brand of dye
- how wet the silk is
- the weight and type of silk
- the type of salt
- the temperature of the salt
- the amount of salt
- the temperature of the room

Salt causes the dye to move as it is soaked into each grain. The grains of

31

Salt-solution sampler

a few grains of salt somehow always find their way on to other parts of the silk, causing marks where they were not wanted.

COVERING MISTAKES

Salt is often useful for correcting mistakes, for example covering up watermarks or hard-edged lines. Salt will not work as well on dye that has been previously dried and re-wetted with water. Therefore, if you are attempting to cover a mistake, it is advisable to re-paint the area with dye before sprinkling with salt.

SALT SOLUTIONS

Another, somewhat less dramatic, texture may be obtained from salt by making it into a solution. When the

Sunflowers. Salt solution

silk is coated in this solution, it helps prevent the dyes from spreading.

To make this solution, stir 250 grams of table salt into one litre of lukewarm water. Stir and leave to dissolve for one hour. Either soak the silk in this solution, then hang it up to dry, or stretch the silk on to the frame and paint the solution on to the silk using a large, soft brush, sponge or cotton wool. When dry, the silk will sparkle with tiny crystals.

When painting the salt-impregnated background, take care to apply only tiny dots of colour. If the brush is overloaded with dye the salt effect will disappear. A 'pointillist' or 'impressionist' type of technique can be used. This background is ideal for small flower pictures: a fairly finely detailed design can be painted, as the dried-salt solution prevents the natural flow of the dyes. Try experimenting and painting on the silk while the solution is still damp. The dye dries in a small scallop or zig-zagged edge, and a small, dainty texture of white spots can be seen.

Sunflowers *(see above)*

This little design was created using the salt-impregnated background. The petals of the sunflowers were painted first. Quick, definite movements with the brush ensure

that the texture of the salt is not lost. The centres were filled with colour using only the tip of the brush. The green and navy stems were formed by quickly wriggling the brush and dye down the silk. The frame was propped up at this stage to aid the running of the dye down the silk.

FIXING

Lastly, the dye needs to be fixed permanently into the silk. The method for doing this will vary, depending on the dyes used. Check the instructions on your dye bottles and see pages 118–21.

TIPS

- Use pongée 5–10 or crêpe de Chine.
- Mix your own dark colours, or use browns, greens or blues.
- Pour dyes into a palette or jar. Take care not to get salt in your dye bottle.
- Paint the silk with water or diluent first.
- Warm the salt.
- Do not use too much salt.
- When using the salt-solution technique, re-paint the background with more salt solution and leave it to dry again if there are not enough small salt dots visible.

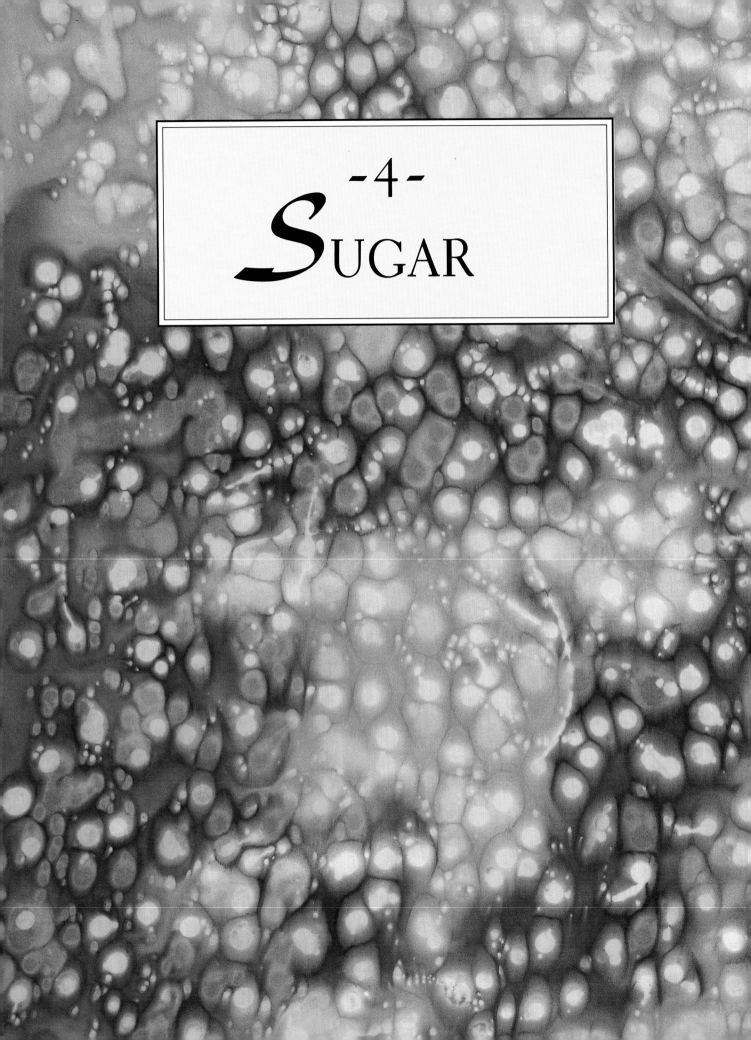

-4-
SUGAR

The sugar technique is not quite as dramatic as the salt technique. Sprinkling sugar granules on to dye-covered silk, while it is still damp, does have a mild effect and will form a texture, but nowhere near as much movement occurs as with salt. Sugar in a thick solution can create some stunning results, however, as it reacts as a resist to the dyes.

This technique involves painting the silk with a thick, syrup-like sugar solution and then adding dye. The solution acts as a resist and tries to stop the flow of the dyes. As it is not an absolute barrier like wax or gutta, the dye slowly creeps in and around the sugar, creating a softer edge. As the silk dries, the dyes are pushed away from the sugar, creating some wonderful textures. The end result is again really beyond your control. The textures obtained can resemble biological cells, marbled effects, galaxies, rain running down a window or the bark of a tree.

These textures are created by the interaction of the sugar, dyes, water and silk. The end result will be different every time, depending especially on how thick the syrup solution has been made. Experiment with this technique. It is quite sticky and messy but great fun.

(*Previous page*)
Cells. Sugar syrup on satin

EQUIPMENT NEEDED

- Silk
- Water
- Icing and granulated sugar
- Frame and pins
- Masking tape
- Dyes
- Brushes and applicators
- Palettes, jars, droppers
- Spray

SUGAR

Icing sugar

Icing sugar is ideal for making up the syrup solution. To make the solution, mix equal quantities of icing sugar and water. Boil the mixture until it is reduced by half. The solution should be fairly thick, with a syrup-like consistency rather like double cream, and it may be used hot or cold. It can be stored in an airtight container in the fridge for several weeks. After a time it will go solid, but it can just be re-heated and made ready for use again, so it does not go to waste.

Granulated sugar

Another option is to make a solution of sugar and lukewarm water (do not boil). Mix one litre of water to 250 grams of sugar. A solution will form immediately, and this can then be painted all over the background of the stretched silk. The sugar granules act as an anti-flow and, when the dyes are painted on to the silk, they do not immediately spread. When the background has been impregnated with the granulated-sugar solution a crusty

texture is formed, which is useful for sand and earth pictures.

SILK

The icing sugar in solution works very well on all types of silk – even the thicker ones – especially satin and heavy crêpe de Chine. Always experiment on a small sample piece to test the reaction.

DYES

The stronger the dye, the better the result. All brands of silk-painting dyes work well with this technique.

THE SUGAR TECHNIQUE

Icing-sugar solution

Stretch the silk tightly on to a frame. Drop the thick syrup solution from a brush or dropper on to the silk. Place lots of blobs of syrup all over the silk in different sizes. While the syrup is still wet, apply the dyes around the syrup blobs (see the cells photograph on pages 34–5). Make sure that the silk is quite wet with dyes around the sugar, until the whole piece of silk is painted (unless you plan to have some white gaps). A spray may also be used to cover the silk with dye.

It is not compulsory to put on the dyes while the syrup is still wet, but a much more interesting texture will develop if you do (see the marbled silk opposite). If the syrup has dried

Painting dye around sugar blobs, with a marbled effect on background painting

Tree bark. Applying the sugar syrup with a stiff brush

into hard lumps a firmer outline will result, similar to that which appears when wax has been used as a resist.

The syrup may also be spattered, dribbled or flicked on to the silk using a toothbrush, nailbrush or even a scrubbing brush. Try putting some syrup solution into a shallow dish, dipping a scrubbing brush or pan-cleaning brush into the syrup and then dragging it across the silk to make a series of lines.

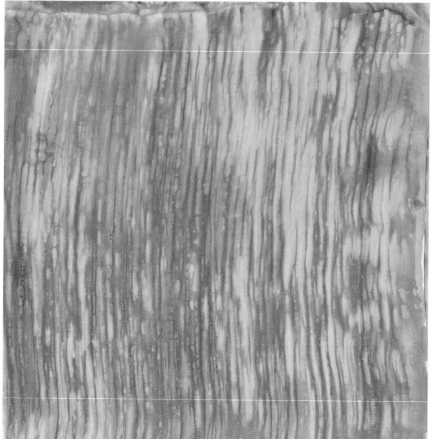

A sponge may also be dipped into the solution and printed on to the silk. You can continue to drip, trail or print more sugar on top of the wet dyes and they will continue to react for some time.

The solution can also be painted on with a small, stiff brush in lines, circles, abstract or flower shapes. These lines will act as a resist.

You can try lifting the frame upright and letting the dye and syrup trickle down the silk. This can be a very messy process: place newspapers under and around your frame. More dye and syrup can be added if needed. This technique is shown in the photograph opposite.

Detail of bark texture

Rain running down a car windscreen.
Created by dripping sugar syrup

The silk may take up to two or three days to dry, depending on the room temperature. The silk will be very stiff and possibly a little sticky. After a while, when the dyes have stopped reacting to the syrup, you can aid drying time with a hairdryer.

Granulated-sugar solution

Stretch the silk tightly on to the frame. Paint the granulated-sugar

Three sugar techniques.
(Back) Resist: paint syrup solution on the silk in stripes with a thick brush. Paint beige and brick-red dye on each side of the wet solution
(Front left) Sprayed satin: trickle sugar solution down the silk. Spray dyes over the surface
(Front right) Sprinkled granules: paint the silk in brown and purple stripes. While damp, sprinkle dry, granulated sugar over the surface

solution on to the background and leave it to dry. When dry, the surface will be less permeable to the water and dye. The sugar crystals produce a crusty texture: this takes quite a time to dry, and removing the crystals is difficult. Sometimes they look rather good left on the silk, especially in a sea or beach scene.

FIXING

The dyes need to be fixed permanently into the silk. The method for this varies, depending on the dyes used. When fixing steam-fixed dyes, use at least a double layer of fixing paper, and try to keep this silk separate from other work. The sugar solution will run out of the fabric and into the fixing water. With all the dyes, make sure that you wash all the solution out of the silk after fixing. See pages 118–21 for further information on fixing methods.

Sugar syrup painted on the background

TIPS

● Use pongée 9, crêpe de Chine, satin or crêpe georgette.
● When steam fixing, use two or more layers of fixing paper.
● Keep left-over sugar solution in an airtight, screwtop jar for further use. Mould developing on the surface can be removed – the syrup is still usable!
● Protect the surface beneath the silk, as the syrup will drip through and is difficult to remove once dry.

-5-
ALCOHOL

Useful for tricks and textures, the alcohol technique is a simple method of adding an extra three-dimensional effect to your work.

Many of the results may look similar to those of the watercolour technique, in that the dyes are pushed away by the alcohol as with the water. The difference can be seen in the stronger reaction of the dyes when alcohol is used. The colour lightens, and the centre becomes clear with the dye pigments building up at the edges, appearing much darker. If this process is repeated several times, the centre becomes increasingly lighter and the outer line more defined.

The alcohol used in these experiments is called *methanol* in Europe, and is readily available in Do-It-Yourself shops. It is used primarily for starting coal or wood fires. This may not be as easily available in Britain, so you may need to look for alternatives. There are several strengths of alcohol: the purer the alcohol, the more effective the result. Pure ethyl alcohol is ideal but may not be available without a permit. This can be diluted with water, and the weaker the solution, the poorer the reaction with the dyes.

Alternatives such as methylated spirit, medicinal alcohol and surgical spirit could be used, and should be available at chemists. Remember that these products are inflammable: they should be used

(Previous page)
Abstract snails on pongée 10

and stored with great care. The silk is not affected by the use of these products, although soaking in them is not recommended.

EQUIPMENT NEEDED

- Silk
- Water
- Alcohol: methanol, ethyl alcohol, methylated spirit, medicinal alcohol or surgical spirit
- Eco-spray or mouth diffuser
- Frame and pins
- Masking tape
- Dyes
- Diluent
- Brushes, applicators, palette, jars
- Cotton wool
- Hairdryer

SILK

Any silk may be used with this technique. Slubbed silk (such as wild silk) will not produce even results due to the irregularities within the weave, however, so uniform dots or circles will be difficult to obtain. A pre-patterned silk such as a jacquard weave will not show this effect to advantage either, as the patterning in the fabric would counteract the texture created by the alcohol.

DYES

The fluid, transparent, steam-fixed dyes always move well when alcohol is applied. Some iron-fixed dyes also produce reasonable results. You will need to experiment prior to using the alcohol on important work. Alcohol can be mixed with the

dyes at the outset of painting. It could be used as an alternative to diluent, helping the smooth, even flow of the dye when painted on to the silk. If a strong, concentrated colour is required, dilute the dye with up to 15 per cent alcohol. Paler colours can be obtained by adding up to 75 per cent alcohol and 25 per cent water to the dye. The more alcohol to water, the more pastel the shade obtained. This method of diluting can only be done economically if you can obtain alcohol easily, probably in the form of methanol.

When using a high percentage of alcohol in the dye, you will notice that the dye covers the silk evenly but that it dries very fast. The alcohol evaporates very quickly, especially on hot days, so you must work fast if you are painting large pieces of silk in this way. Alcohol has the opposite effect to diluent, which wets the fabric, allowing the dyes to spread evenly over a longer period of time.

There are some dye colours which do not react as well as others to alcohol. If you wish to use this technique, you must test the dyes beforehand on a similar piece of silk. Re-application of the alcohol two or three times can often continue and increase the effect of poorer colours.

BRUSHES AND APPLICATORS

There are many successful ways of applying alcohol to the silk, including the use of fine, thick and fan-shaped brushes, cotton wool and cotton buds, sprays (including mouth diffusers), Eco-spray and airbrush.

Spirals on a colour wheel

CREATING TEXTURE WITH ALCOHOL

The following examples show the exciting results which may be used on small, selected areas of your work or on large expanses of silk which they can cover quickly.

Placing dots on a plain background

The reaction of the alcohol is clearly seen in the above demonstration. Stretch the silk on to a frame and paint it with dye. Dry thoroughly with a hairdryer, or a crisp, definite shape will not appear.

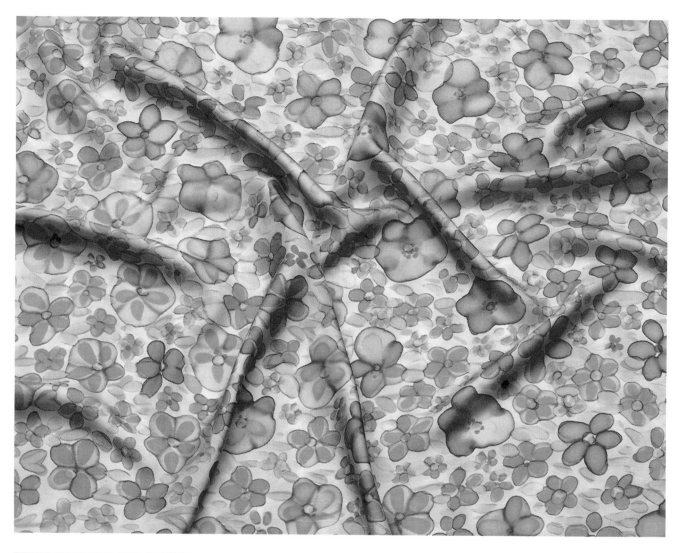

Flower fantasy

Dip a cotton bud into the alcohol and tap the excess out on to absorbent tissue paper. The more alcohol on the bud, the larger the circle that will be made. A fine brush may be used with similar results. The dye pigments will be pushed away by gently rubbing the surface of the silk, and some of the dye will be absorbed on to the cotton bud and removed from the silk. Use new cotton buds to continue applying the alcohol.

Allow the silk to dry. If a larger circle or stronger reaction is needed, re-apply the alcohol: the stronger the dye, the greater the reaction will be.

An even pattern can be built up by doing this, and the texture can make a plain, flat area much more interesting. Backgrounds which have been painted unevenly with dye can also be camouflaged in this way.

Flower fantasy (*see above*)

Paint a wash of lilac dye over the stretched silk. Allow this to dry thoroughly, and then paint petalled flowers in a stronger purple all over the surface. Try to vary the size of the flowers and the strength of the dye to add interest. Allow the flowers

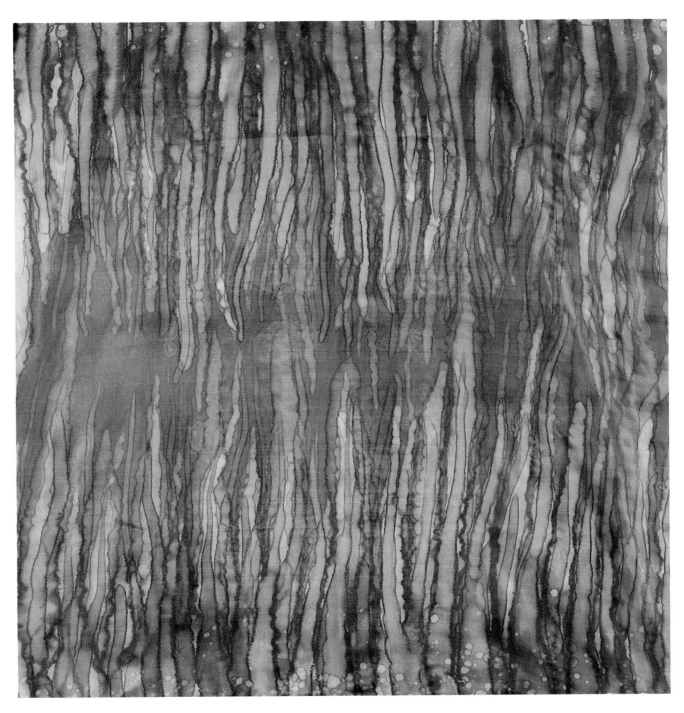

Stalactites

to dry before painting the stalks and leaves. Again, allow these to dry, and finally dot dark brown into the centres of the larger flowers to create a focal point.

Dip a fine brush into the alcohol and place it over the flower shapes. Flatten the brush on the silk so that the oval of the petal is formed. The flowers will immediately spread, their petals overlapping: this is the effect you are trying to achieve. Do the same with the leaf shapes, and finally the flower centres. The result looks like a carpet of flowers strewn over the silk.

USING BRUSHES TO CREATE LINES

Stalactites *(see previous page)*

The casual, random effect of these lines is created by painting the background with a strong, dark brown dye. Dry the silk and prop the frame up vertically. Use a medium-sized brush to trickle alcohol on to the silk from the outer edge towards the centre. Repeat this over and over again. Turn the frame, and complete the other side in the same manner. The dyes will be pushed to the edges of the stripes, forming uneven and varied shades of brown on the silk.

Formal stripes *(see right)*

Paint bands of alcohol as evenly as possible over the background. The results will be much more 'formal' than the stalactite dripping, yet still make a pleasing texture. A whole scarf can be built up using this method over different background colours. A landscape with ploughed fields can also be enhanced by stripes of alcohol.

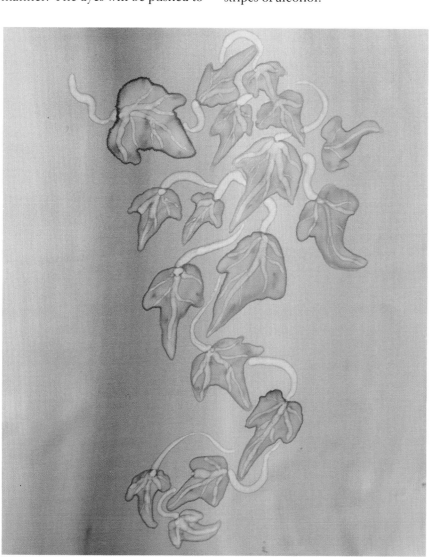

Ivy leaves *(see left)*

Paint the background with a wash of pale brown and allow to dry. Paint the ivy leaves freely on top in shades of green and yellow, using a fine brush so that the leaves do not spread too far. Dip the tip of the brush into alcohol and lightly paint the veins of the leaves and the stems on the background colour. Do not overload the brush: dab off the excess on to absorbent tissue paper.

Ivy leaves. Use of alcohol to show veins and stems

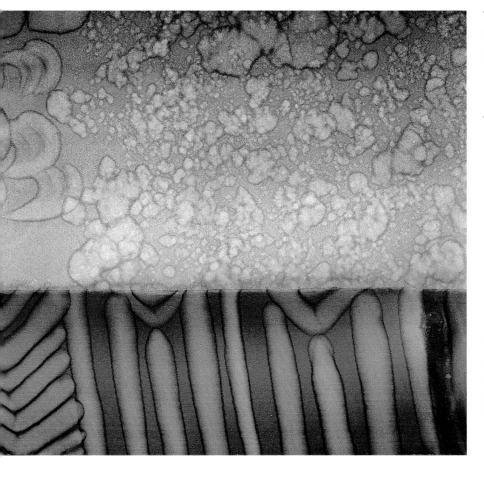

Sampler of alcohol techniques.
(Top left) Sponging
(Top right) Spraying
(Bottom left) Brushing
(Bottom right) Formal stripes

ALTERNATIVE METHODS OF APPLYING ALCOHOL

Spraying

Use a mouth diffuser or Eco-spray to create a spatter effect. An airbrush is of no use as the spray is too fine.

Sponging

Stipple the surface with a sponge. Press heavily to emphasize the texture, but be careful not to over-saturate the sponge before pressing it on to the silk.

Cotton wool

Several effects may be created using cotton wool.

- Swirl and dab distant clouds to produce an uneven texture.
- Pull a pad of cotton wool horizontally across the surface to form stripes.
- Make blocks of alcohol marks by placing the pad of cotton wool quickly on the surface.
- Use quick, curved movements for circles.
- Pads of cotton wool soaked in alcohol will remove large amounts of dye from the silk. This is useful for lightening dye that is too dark or has been applied unevenly.
- Try using a cotton-wool bud to produce circles of uniform size.

TIPS

- Use cotton buds and alcohol to remove dye from silk: leakages and splashes can often be taken out in this way. Simply place a pad of cotton wool under the mistake and, using a cotton bud dipped in alcohol, rub the area gently. The dye will be lightened in colour, if not completely removed. Remember to block the hole in a gutta line before trying to remove the leaked dye.
- Keep a large container ready with 75 per cent alcohol and 25 per cent water, for diluting the dyes. Plastic squash bottles are ideal.
- Store all inflammable liquids carefully.
- Do not inhale for long periods of time. Work with adequate ventilation.

-6-
WAX

The process of applying molten wax and dyes is traditionally known as *batik*. This is usually a long process which involves immersing the fabric completely in a dye bath. In this chapter we will show you how to use wax as a resist, painted directly on to the fabric with the silk paints and dyes. This is far less time-consuming than traditional methods, and a great variety of colours, designs and textures can be obtained. Transparent dyes lend themselves well to this technique, as the colours can be over-painted to create further colours.

With traditional batik it is always necessary to keep to a colour plan. The lightest colour must be dyed first, and every successive colour influences the one before (for example, if the first colour is yellow and the second is blue, the result will be not blue but green). For this reason it is impossible to obtain red and green without dry cleaning and re-waxing. With the direct-painting method, however, these colour combinations are possible.

The cracking effect that is so characteristic of batik can still be obtained, and it is fun to experiment with all the different methods of applying wax and all the textures which can be created.

Rainbow on pongée 9

EQUIPMENT NEEDED

- Silk
- Wax
- Wax brushes, tjantings, tjaps
- Heater
- Frame and pins
- Masking tape
- Dyes
- Palette, jars, dye brushes
- Iron and ironing-board
- Newsprint or brown paper

WAX

The wax used for this technique is a mixture of paraffin wax and beeswax. Paraffin wax is white and may be bought in blocks, beads or in powder form. It is cheap, very hard and good for the cracking technique (see pages 60–1). Candles may also be used. Beeswax is more expensive than paraffin wax and is yellow in colour. Pure beeswax is soft, and is useful if no cracking is required or if fine, detailed work is needed.

The best mixture to use is ¾ paraffin wax to ¼ beeswax. If too much paraffin wax is used, it will crack too much and may peel off, allowing the dye to encroach on areas where it is not required.

Another option is to use a ready-prepared batik wax. This is available in granulated or bead form and is of course ideal for this technique.

Heating the wax

The wax may be heated in a thermostatically-controlled wax pot, a frying pan, or a double boiler. Wax and its fumes are highly inflammable, and great care must be taken not to overheat it: the wax needs to keep a constant temperature

51

of 120°C. This is easy to do if you have a wax pot, and it is really worth buying one of these if you intend to use wax frequently (see the list of suppliers on pages 123–5).

As the wax is applied to the silk, it should leave a transparent line. If the wax sits on the surface of the silk and looks hard and white, it has not penetrated the fibres of the silk and will not become a barrier for the dye. If the wax has been allowed to overheat, it will run and spread too far and your wax brushes will be quickly ruined.

SILK

All silks work well with this technique. If a heavy crackle is required, wild silk and a heavy crêpe de Chine produce good results.

If the silk is very thick you may need to apply wax on both sides. Thicker silk may require a hotter wax temperature for thorough penetration.

DYES

All the brands of silk paints and dyes can be used with wax. Transparent dyes are particularly effective, but they all produce excellent results.

WAX BRUSHES

Quality is not really an important consideration when choosing wax brushes. The constant heat of the

Wax lines produced with various tools, brushes and applicators. From left to right:
single tjanting
triple tjanting
fan-shaped brush
fine brush and toothbrush
flat-headed brush
comb
tjap

Brushing wax on to coloured silk

melted wax tends to shorten the life of any brush, especially if the wax overheats. Flat-headed bristle brushes, fan brushes, squirrel-hair and household painting brushes are all ideal for use with wax. If a large plain area is required, a household or flat-headed bristle brush will do very well. If an area of non-textured colour is required, spread the wax thickly or apply two coats on the front and back of the silk.

A very stiff bristle brush can create a fine linear texture, as shown in the photograph on pages 50–1. A fine spattered effect may be obtained by flicking the tip of a bristle brush against the end of your finger, or a ruler or brush handle. Protect areas that do not require spattering with polythene or thick paper.

Varying-width lines of wax may be achieved depending on the brush used (brushes can be trimmed to any shape you require). Try to keep a fine sable brush just for more delicate and intricate work.

TJANTINGS

A tjanting (sometimes called a canting) is a special tool for applying wax. It can also be used for drawing fine lines on the wax. The tjanting is a small copper bowl attached to a wooden handle with one or more spouts leading from its base.

Tjantings are available with up to six different-sized spouts, which produce lines of varying thickness.

TJAPS AND OTHER APPLICATORS

Wax can also be applied to silk with cotton buds, homemade metal printing blocks and tjaps. A tjap is a copper printing block mounted on wood. It is commonly found in Indonesia and is used for repeat designs.

THE WAX TECHNIQUE

The silk can be stretched over a frame (it is not compulsory for this technique, but it is easier). Stretch the silk evenly and tightly, or it will pucker after the wax has dried and the dye will not be able to spread evenly. Heat the wax and keep the wax container as close to your work as possible.

Painting direct

This technique is sometimes rather difficult to grasp. The wax is applied to the areas of silk which are to remain white before the silk is painted. When the dye is dry, more wax may be applied. Cover the areas of colour you wish to keep as they are with wax, and then paint again. The beauty of this technique is that this process of direct painting can be repeated as many times as required, until a wonderful variety of colours has been produced.

In the rainbow-slashes photograph on pages 50–1, the white linear textures were applied using wax and a stiff bristle brush. The rainbow of colours was then painted. Wax was applied again over the rainbow of colours before the whole piece of silk was painted black.

Spattered wax

Bacon. False batik

In the rainbow ovals on the previous page the silk was painted first with red, green, yellow, blue, purple and indigo. The ovals were applied in wax with a squirrel-hair brush and the silk was then painted black.

False batik

A traditional 'look' may be obtained by layering the colours, starting with the lightest and painting over the complete piece of silk after each waxing instead of dipping in a dye bath. This technique is sometimes known as _faux_ or _false batik_. You must plan your colours in advance so that you can add them in the correct order. You must start with the lightest colour first, and progress through to the darkest colour. It is a good idea to make a sample strip to test your dyes as you paint.

When the dyes are painted on top of each other, they mix to create a new colour. When green is painted over red, for example, a brown is obtained. When blue is painted over a yellow, green and black colour scheme, but you would like some red berries, you can paint the berries on first and then cover them in wax.

Use of tjantings

The tjanting is dipped into the hot wax so that the wax fills the copper bowl. The liquid wax is then applied to the fabric through the spout or spouts. Electric tjantings are available: these keep the wax temperature constant so that the spouts do not become blocked with hardened wax. When using these, however, one must get used to working with the electrical wire constantly attached.

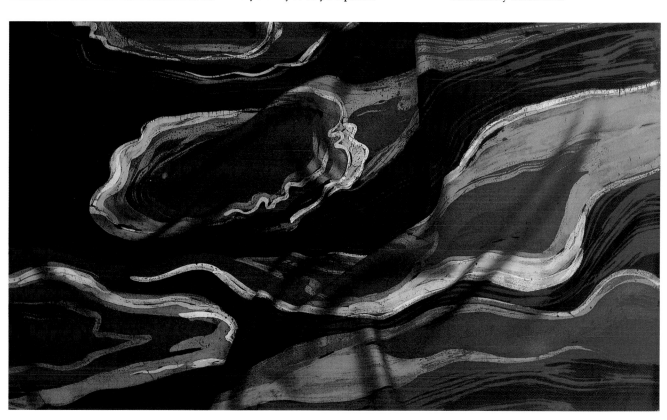

Use of a triple tjanting

Intricate tjanting work

When working with a tjanting, leave the reservoir in the hot wax for a few seconds to allow the copper bowl to heat. Try to keep the liquid wax at an even level in the reservoir. While transferring the tjanting full of hot wax to the silk, cover the spout with a tissue or cotton wool to prevent wax from dripping on to the silk. Wipe the underside of the bowl frequently to remove excess wax.

Trail the spout across the silk, without pressing too hard. The trail of wax will vary in size depending on how fast you are moving the tjanting and the heat of the wax. If the wax is at the correct temperature, a fine, even, transparent line will appear. If the wax is too hot it will spread too far. Long, flowing lines may be achieved with a tjanting, and it is also capable of small, intricate designs.

Sometimes the wax solidifies in the spout and it becomes blocked. If this happens, clean the spout with a fine wire or leave it in the hot wax for a few minutes.

When the tjanting work is finished, the dyes can be painted directly on to the silk. Unless you are an expert with a tjanting, bear in mind, when deciding on a tjanting design, that the design may have to be adapted at times to cover any misplaced drops of wax that may fall on to the silk.

Use of other applicators

The tjap is not dipped into the molten wax, but pressed on to a wax-soaked pad before being printed on to the silk. Try making your own metal block: a coil of wire or even a potato masher can be used.

Flowing tjanting work

Tjap print

Printing with a potato masher

(Previous page)
Cracking techniques. From left to right:
   radiating (orange and yellow)
   one-colour cracking (red)
   multi-coloured cracking (yellow, green,
   blue)
   pleated cracking (purple)

For the potato-masher print (above) the silk was painted yellow first. The potato masher was heated in the molten wax and stamped on to the silk. The silk was then painted green. When dry, it was printed again and painted black.

The flower tjap print on page 57 (bottom) uses the same method as above. Do not overload the fine wires with wax. Print on to a piece of paper to remove excess wax, and place firmly on the silk. The silk does not need to be stretched on to a frame, but laid over a padded, flat surface. When cooled, it is covered with a wash of colour.

Cracking

The characteristic texture created by cracking the wax can enhance your work. Depending on your design, you may need to 'crack' certain areas only or the whole piece. As soon as the wax has dried it can be cracked. The wax must be completely dry and hard before crumpling: if it is still malleable it will not crack. Try putting it in the fridge: this will soon harden the wax.

To obtain the crackles, remove the silk from the frame and crumple it in your hands. Now lay it on some paper or pin it back on to the frame.

ironing-board with an old sheet and layers of paper. It is difficult – in fact impossible – to remove all the wax in this way. If you have used steam-fixed dyes, more wax will be removed during the fixing process. Sometimes after the ironing procedure a faint grease line is still visible and the silk still feels stiff. If this is the case, the silk can be soaked in white spirit to remove remaining wax or dry cleaned.

Paint the silk with dye. If you hold the silk up to the light you can see whether the dye is penetrating the cracks. If it is not doing so, rub the surface with dye using a cotton-wool pad. It is difficult to determine the end result at this stage, and care must be taken not to over-crackle. On pale, intricate work the dye may penetrate too thoroughly and ruin the design, but large, over-bright backgrounds can be subdued by cracking.

Controlled cracking

It is possible to control the cracking to a certain extent, by folding and pleating the silk in certain directions rather than simply crumpling it haphazardly. It is possible to achieve several colour crackings by coating

each set of cracks with wax before re-cracking and re-dyeing.

Removal of wax

Most of the wax can be removed from the silk by ironing it between layers of absorbent paper. Do not use newspapers next to your silk as the newsprint will sometimes reprint on to it (very old newspapers are usually satisfactory, however, as the newsprint is thoroughly dry). Try to use brown paper, kraft paper or lining paper for this job. The paper left over from steam fixing can also be used.

As the wax melts under the heat of the iron it will be absorbed by the paper. Keep replacing the saturated paper with clean layers until as much wax as possible has been removed. Remember to protect your

TIPS

● Make sure that the wax is hot enough.
● Hold a tissue or a piece of cotton wool in your hand to catch drips of wax.
● Re-coat the silk with wax if it begins to flake after several layers of dye.
● If the wax has not penetrated the silk, turn it over and wax again on the other side.
● Open the window when waxing, especially when ironing out wax.
● Use two or three layers of fixing paper when steam fixing to absorb the wax.
● Do not put the hairdryer too near the wax when fast-drying the dye or it will melt.
● Never wax while the silk is still damp, as the wax will not penetrate the silk thoroughly.

-7-
Gutta

Most silk painters will have been introduced to the gutta technique, one of the important skills that should be mastered when silk painting. Here we will show you many more ways of applying the resist to create imaginative textures and styles.

EQUIPMENT NEEDED

- Silk
- Gutta: solvent-based, water-based, coloured, metallic or permanent
- Solvents: Essence F or white spirit
- Typographic ink or stained-glass colour
- Nibs, pipettes, cones
- Rollers, sponges
- Frame and pins
- Dyes and brushes
- Masking tape
- Cotton wool
- Hairdryer

GUTTA (SERTI)

There are two types of gutta: solvent-based and water-based. The latter has the advantage that it can be removed from the silk by simply washing in soap and water. The gutta can be bought in applicators which have their own spouts, which are useful for children.

If the gutta is too thick to penetrate the silk, water can be added to thin down the product

Dripped gold gutta and Essence F mix on pongée 9

(solvent-based guttas can prove more difficult to bring to the correct consistency). Always check the manufacturer's instructions and thin using the recommended product.

Both types of gutta have to be used correctly to create a good resist to the dyes. Take care not to paint over the outlines, or the dyes may be absorbed into them. The water-based gutta may become soggy if a wash of dyes is painted over it, and it also goes sticky in a steamer or when used with liquid-fixed dyes. Solvent-based gutta does not have these problems, but it does suffer from evaporation and thickening.

Many metallic and coloured guttas have recently been developed. There are products which remain in the silk even after dry cleaning: these are called permanent guttas. Remember that gutta remaining in the silk will always have a rubbery feel along the gutta lines or textures. Although more expensive, coloured guttas (sold in small bottles) are useful in providing interesting surface texture. It is also possible to make your own colours by adding stained-glass colour or typographic ink to ordinary clear gutta. To do this, mix a small amount of colour with the appropriate thinning agent (Essence F or white spirit) and then add it to the colourless gutta. Shake thoroughly before use.

Metallic guttas are very attractive and can add sparkle and life to your work, but the small particles within the gutta tend to clog nibs and often cause frustration. The 'glittery' gold and silver types seem to cause quite a few problems, and even disappear after frequent washing. Always test guttas before using them on a special piece of work, and check on their

Swirling red gutta applied by cone
(see below and overleaf)

washing and dry-cleaning instructions. If you are in doubt, wash your silk items by hand.

TRADITIONAL USE OF GUTTA

A brief explanation of the traditional method of using gutta is necessary before you embark on the more experimental exercises.

The purpose of the gutta line is to penetrate the fibres of the silk to create a barrier which is waterproof and therefore dye-proof. When dye is painted on to the silk, it will naturally flow along the warp and weft of the fabric. The fine lines of gutta prevent the dye from spreading, allowing a controlled design to be painted.

The detailed patterns on the Egyptian scarf shown opposite use a black gutta to form the outlines. Jewel-bright colours are then boldly painted into these shapes. The motifs stand out from each other as clear pools of colour.

SOLVENTS

It is very important for this technique that the consistency of the gutta is correct. If the gutta is too thick, it will sit on the surface of the fabric; if too thin, the barrier will not be dye-proof. Try a test piece before you begin, to check that the gutta is flowing correctly. Add solvents (Essence F or white spirit) or water, a drop at a time, to thin the liquid down. More experimental use of thinned gutta will be discussed later in the chapter (see pages 70–1).

NIBS, PIPETTES AND CONES

Gutta is either stored in its own applicator, complete with spout, or can be decanted from a larger bottle into a plastic pipette. A waxed-paper cone is often used by professionals, but can be rather messy.

The thickness of the gutta outline depends very much on the size of the cone or spout opening. A fine

Traditional gutta work on Egyptian-design scarf, using black gutta and pipette

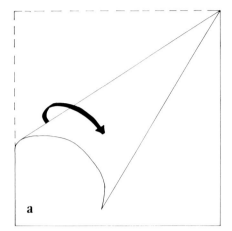

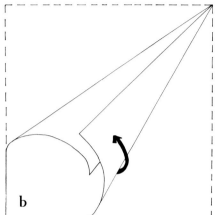

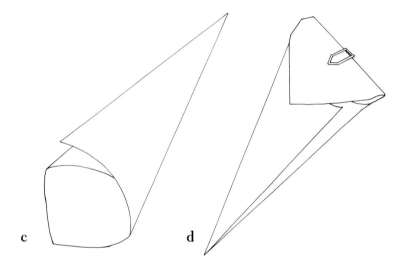

Method of making a cone from greaseproof paper

needle will pierce the spout for a medium-sized line. A neater, finer line can be achieved by attaching a nomographic nib to the spout. The flow of gutta can be regulated by the size of the nib: these are available in different sizes from no. 4 to no. 9 (the lower the number, the finer the hole). Nos. 5 and 6 are usually used. These are either attached to the spout with masking tape, or inserted from inside the screw-on cap. Different makes may vary.

The use of a cone and gutta can be seen in the swirling red-gutta sample on page 64. The fast-flowing circles and overlapping forms with varied widths show that speed is necessary. Vary the pressure on the cone to increase or decrease the thickness of the gutta lines. Allow the gutta to dry thoroughly so that the lines solidify (a hairdryer can speed up this stage). Check for gaps in the gutta by holding the frame up to the light. Your work is now ready for painting. Keep the gutta bottle handy to block up any holes.

SILK

Most types of silk may be used with the gutta technique. Obviously, the thicker the silk, the more difficult it will be for the gutta to resist the dyes, and it may be necessary to apply gutta on both sides of the silk to achieve thorough penetration.

DYES

Any type of dye may be used for painting. Be careful not to flood the gutta areas with too much dye, or the barriers created by the gutta will be broken down. Any part of your work that has dye bleeding through shows that there is either a fault in the gutta line, or that, when painting, the brush tip has gone over the line accidentally. Try to stop the flow of the dye as quickly as possible: soak up the excess with a cotton bud and dry quickly with a hairdryer. Block up the hole and, when dry, continue painting.

Gutta is normally applied to a white background, but the silk can be painted first and the gutta applied afterwards. The Aboriginal motif scarf shown opposite is an example of this effect. Peach, yellow and grey tones form a background wash, and the gutta motifs are applied when the silk is dry. The shapes are painted in stronger, vivid colours. After fixing, the gutta is removed either by dry cleaning or Essence F. The background colours are revealed without any trace of a white gutta line. A thick nib gives a greater effect.

Aboriginal cave-painting motifs

EXPERIMENTING WITH GUTTA

Do not think of gutta as an outliner only. It is a resist, and can be used in the same way as wax, with, in many cases, similar results.

Brushing on gutta

Any brush that is used with gutta will need careful cleaning afterwards. It is preferable to keep several old brushes of different sizes for this method. Pour the gutta on to

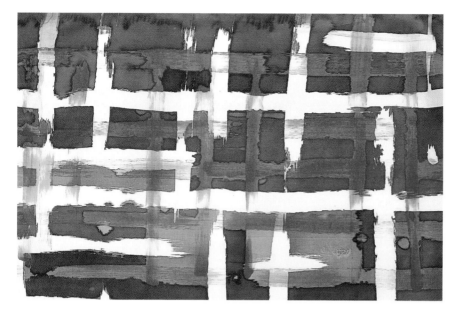

Red and clear gutta painted on with a brush

a palette or a saucer rather than trying to dip into the bottle.

Haphazard application with a brush can take the form of streaking, pulling along or dabbing the surface of the silk. The brush covered with gutta will mark the silk, forming resist areas.

Gold gutta applied over painted flowers

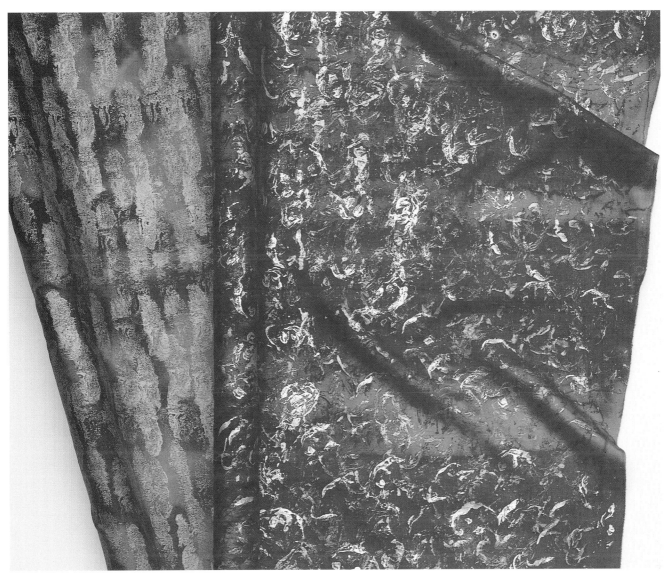

Sponged gold gutta and rolled red, gold and silver gutta samples

Vertical and horizontal stripes of clear gutta are shown in the sample opposite (top), with red and orange dye painted around the textures. A second application of red gutta is added using strong brushstrokes, and the remaining spaces are over-painted with dark blue. The dye creeping in and around the gutta stripes forms the texture.

The second brushed piece (opposite, bottom) shows gold gutta applied after the dyes. Bright colours of orange, red and pink are loosely painted in flower shapes, followed by two-tone leaves in green. Gold gutta, applied with a soft brush, adds definition to the flowers. The whole effect is bright and charming.

Sponging and rag- and paper-rolling

These are extremely simple ways of texturing fabric. Paint the silk in bright washes of red and orange dye.

Pour the thick gold gutta into a saucer, and dip in a small piece of sponge (the edge of a household sponge gives a strong vertical pattern of gold colour on the design shown above [left], but a natural or foam sponge cut into shapes will give very different results).

Rolled and crumpled newspaper can be pressed on to a coloured background. Gold, red and silver guttas are shown in the right-hand sample above. Do not overload the sponge, newspaper or old rags, or the textured effect will be lost.

69

The dyes can be fixed before the application of the guttas, removing the possibility of the fixing paper sticking to the gutta.

Spattering, splashing and graffiti

This is a wild way of covering fabric. Really enjoy yourself with this method. Little talent is needed here – just enthusiasm and a lot of newspaper to cover your work area. Ending up with blobs of gutta everywhere is not ideal! The frame will need to be propped up to allow the gutta to trickle down. This is a useful way of using up old gutta which may have lost its permeability.

Old brushes, sticks or tooth-brushes may be used to flick the gutta on to the silk. The coverage depends very much on the elasticity of the gutta: if it is too thick, only large blobs will be jerked off the brush or stick; if it is too runny, a spread of droplets will occur. The dyes will mingle to a small extent when used with runny, water-based gutta.

Adding solvent or water to gutta

Gutta can still retain its impenetrable elastic property but become much more liquid if dilutant is added to it. In the case of solvent-based gutta, this could be Essence F or white spirit, and for water-based gutta, a few drops of water could be added.

In the example shown on pages 62–3, gold gutta mixed 5:1 with Essence F is trickled over a vertical piece of silk. The gold covers most of

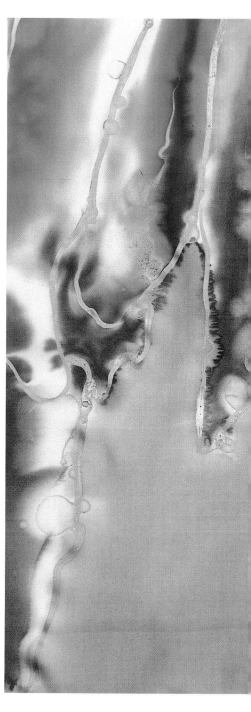

Splashing and graffiti using coloured guttas

A wet background with silver gutta applied direct from a pipette

the fuchsia-painted background in a fine, shimmering layer. The navy dye highlights the spaces. Notice that the gutta base has travelled further in this runny state than the gold particles. A second edge of clear resistance has been formed against the blue dye.

Gutta poured into a wet background will also give an interesting result, as the gutta will spread out over the surface. If dye colour and water are then flicked on to the gutta, the lines will spread out rather like petrol reflected on water: a most unusual effect.

TIPS

● The traditional gutta technique requires practice. Stretch up a small piece of silk to test the gutta consistency and the nib size.

● Remove any bracelets or turn back loose cuffs of blouses to prevent smudging of a gutta line.

● Remove smudged gutta immediately with a cotton bud dipped in a solvent such as Essence F or white spirit, or water. A new product called 'gutta remover' has just become available (see the list of suppliers on pages 123–5).

● Shake bottles of metallic gutta well before use, as the particles settle to the bottom of the bottle. Use a fine wire to unblock the nib when particles lodge and block it up.

● Use 'permanent' gold or silver if you intend to dry-clean or wash an article frequently.

71

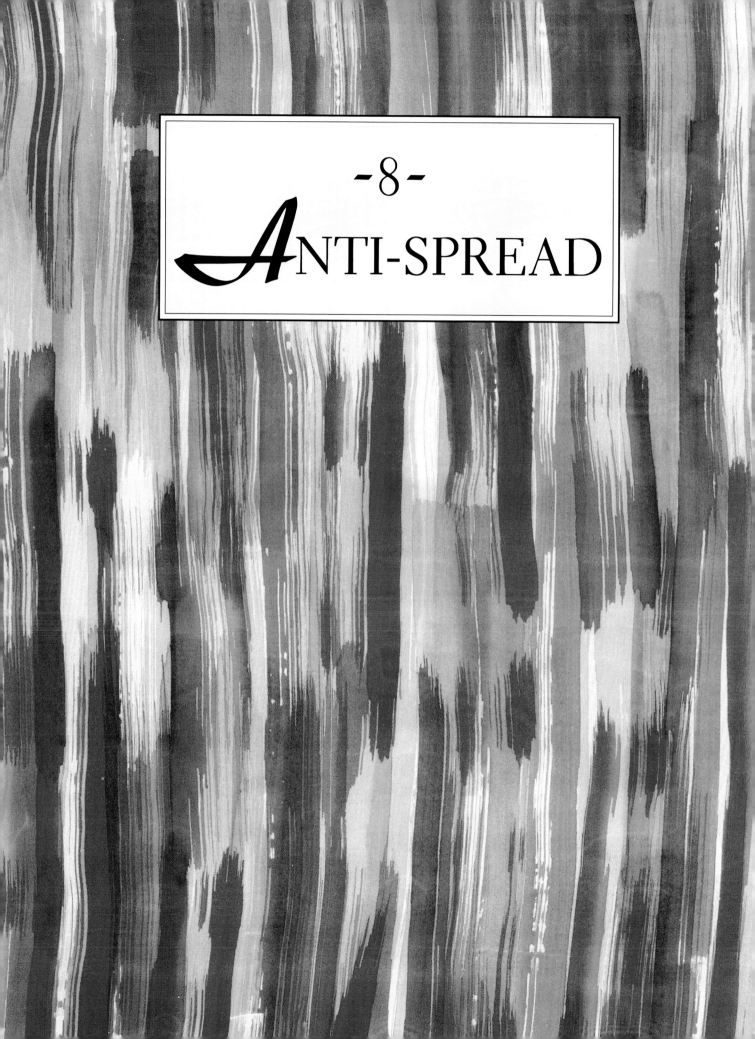

-8-
ANTI-SPREAD

The purpose of anti-spread is to stop the dye moving freely across the silk. It is a form of resist that is applied either to the whole piece of silk, or to specific areas where fine detail is needed. Its effect is that the dyes do not penetrate fully into the silk throughout the fibres. The Chinese used a form of antifusant on their traditional paintings: layer on layer of rice water was coated over the surface of the silk to prevent the dyes from spreading.

Anti-spread can be found in specialist silk-painting shops (see pages 123–5). It is marketed under several names (depending on the manufacturer) such as stop-flow, antifusant and anti-spread. Should you not be able to find it, there are various alternatives. These have been mentioned briefly in other chapters, but deserve a more thorough explanation as very different effects can be created with each.

(Previous page)
Colour painted on top of colour

Oriental trees on pongée 9

Chart showing the effect of different types of anti-spread on crêpe de Chine.
(Top left) No anti-spread
(Top right) Essence F or spirit-based antifusant
(Centre left) Salt-water solution
(Centre right) Sugar syrup
(Bottom left) Hairspray
(Bottom right) Wax and Essence F

EQUIPMENT NEEDED

- Silk
- Anti-spread, antifusant or stop-flow (alternatives: gutta, Essence F, salt, sugar, thickener, wax, starch, hairspray)
- Frame and pins
- Dyes
- Masking tape
- Brushes and sponges
- Cotton wool
- Straws

RESISTING METHODS

The spread of the dye on to and into the silk can be inhibited by using one or several of the following:

(a) different types of silk
(b) water instead of diluent
(c) iron-fixed dyes
(d) solvent-based antifusant: gutta and Essence F
(e) water-based antifusant: water and gutta
(f) salt-and-water solution
(g) sugar-and-water solution and syrup
(h) thickener or *épaissisant*
(i) starch-and-water solution
(j) wax-and-Essence F solution
(k) hairspray

SILK

A silk which resists the spread of the dye can be painted directly using fine brushes and a little dye and water.

A crêpe de Chine, mousseline or crêpe georgette is ideal for use with this technique. In these fabrics, the yarn is twisted during manufacture, producing a 'crimp'. It is this twist which stops the dye from spreading as quickly on the silk as on a smooth silk such as pongée. When painting directly on to these fabrics you will notice that the brush needs to work the dye into the fibres more. The silk will not resist the dye completely, but a more definite pattern can be painted. Examples of this can be seen in Chapter One.

The thickness of the silk must also be taken into consideration: a heavier-weight crêpe de Chine will resist much more than a fine one. Wild silk, because of its thickness, will also resist the dye, although unfortunately the unevenness of the yarn will sometimes allow the dyes to run unexpectedly.

DYES AND THICKENER

Look at the types of dye on the market when trying this technique. We have found that transparent silk-painting dyes are much more liquid than the iron-fixed dyes (the iron-fixed dyes do not move over the silk as freely).

There is no need to add diluent to the dyes and water in this technique, as you are trying to inhibit the flow rather than aiding it.

Obtaining the correct anti-spread consistency. From left to right:
    far too much gutta
    too much gutta
    a perfect mix
    too little gutta

USING ANTI-SPREAD

There are two ways of applying anti-spread. Either coat the required area with a cotton pad soaked in the liquid, or immerse the silk into a bowl of liquid and hang it up to dry. The second method will coat the fibres but may result in an uneven resistance. The first method is more economical, as the silk is stretched ready for use on the frame and can be coated where necessary.

Do not use a brush to paint on the anti-spread if the resist is gutta-based, as the hairs will become clogged.

Solvent-based anti-spread (antifusant)

This product is available ready-prepared, but it is possible to make your own anti-spread by mixing Essence F and spirit-based gutta together. We suggest six parts Essence F to one part gutta (the higher the proportion of gutta, the more resistant the silk becomes to the dye). Pour the Essence F and gutta into an airtight, non-permeable container and shake thoroughly. Always test your antifusant before use to make sure that it has soaked into the silk sufficiently to resist.

After the application of anti-spread the silk must be dried before painting (the drying time can be shortened by using a hairdryer). The Essence F evaporates, leaving a fine, colourless layer of gutta on the surface, and the silk, if already painted, remains bright and translucent underneath. Layer upon layer of dye can now be painted on to the surface. The translucent qualities will remain if the diluted colour is placed on top of darker tones, creating subtle three-dimensional effects.

The best results are achieved with solvent-based antifusant, as crisp, sharp, clear detailing can be painted on to the surface without the colours running. The other methods form a resist, but their results are never as well-defined. Take care when using this product, as it is inflammable. It should only be used in a well-ventilated room.

(Opposite) Eye detail

Water-based anti-spread

This can also be bought ready-prepared or can be made up by diluting water-based gutta to the correct consistency.

A much softer outline results with this type of anti-spread, as the dyes are resisted to a certain extent but not completely. The subtle fused outline can be used to advantage with watercolour painting.

Dripping dyes down the frame

Do not saturate the surface with a wash of dye, as this anti-spread will not resist a great deal of water and the gutta resist will be broken down.

Salt-and-water solution

Dissolve salt in water (as for a salt-impregnated background: see pages 32–3), and paint it over the surface of the silk. Dry immediately with a hairdryer so that the salt crystals do not have a chance to form. The solution will have thickened the silk, and, when the surface is painted,

movement of the dye is stopped. As with the water-based resist, the outline is not crisp. The salt also creates textures of its own with the wet dye.

Sugar solution and sugar syrup

Two methods of preparing this anti-spread have been described in Chapter Four (see page 36). Both can be used to coat the background and will form a resist to dye, although the sugar syrup is rather difficult to apply over large areas.

You should expect some uneven results. The dyes do not look as strong after painting on the syrup, but some unusual textures will form.

Thickener or *épaissisant*

This can also be mixed with the dyes to allow painting without running. The thickener is very difficult to paint evenly on to the surface as the brushstrokes cannot be disguised. A small amount of thickener is stirred into the dye in the palette. This can be very useful for painting details such as faces, branches or leaves.

Starch-and-water solution

Starch powder and water are mixed together to form a thin, milky liquid. This is then painted on to the surface of the silk with a brush. The results are not excellent, but the dyes are resisted to a certain extent.

Wax-and-Essence F solution

This can be used as a resist but has a greasy feel, and the silk will need thorough cleaning in white spirit after fixing. Only average results will be achieved and, if other methods are available, you will find them easier to use.

Add wax granules to Essence F and stir until dissolved. A white, milky solution will eventually be formed. Apply the liquid to the surface of the silk using a pad of cotton wool.

Blowing dyes over the silk surface

Hairspray

Amazingly good results can be achieved with hairspray. Spray over the surface of the silk until it is thoroughly saturated. Wait until the silk has dried and then paint as usual.

TECHNIQUES USING ANTI-SPREAD BACKGROUNDS

Most of the samples in this chapter were created using solvent-based anti-spread. As we have explained, this gives a sharp definition to the edges of the dyes.

Dripping and pouring

Coat the background with anti-spread and dry thoroughly. Then simply trickle bright colours down an upright frame so that the dye courses freely down the silk. Dry the silk after each application of colour to stop them from fusing with each other. Tones underneath paler ones will show through.

Blowing

The photograph on page 74 illustrates this method (the blowing technique is also shown below). Paint a bright circular background wash, using diluent with the dyes to

help them merge evenly. When dry, coat the surface with anti-spread. Place the frame flat on a table and drip dyes on to the surface of the silk. Using a straw, blow these blobs over the silk to create spidery branches. Finally, tip up the frame, allowing the remaining dye to course down the silk. A brush may be used to widen the bands.

Landscape painting

Detailed pictures may be built up after anti-spread has been applied. The landscape shown here demonstrates the use of two techniques. Diluent and pale-colour wash is used first to create the sky and water reflections; then the surface is coated with anti-spread. The mountain forms are added, drying between each colour application to keep them separate. Next, the land mass and reflection detailing is added, and finally the bamboos in the foreground are sharply defined.

> **TIPS**
>
> ● A slight 'shadow' from the anti-spread will mark your work if it is applied to a small area. This can be removed after fixing by placing the silk in white spirit or by dry cleaning.
> ● Take care not to leave any gaps when applying anti-spread, as these will result in dye spreading to unwanted areas. Apply the anti-spread methodically.
> ● Test the anti-spread before starting on an inconspicuous area. If the dye still spreads, re-coat lightly.

Landscape. Use of antifusant when painting details

81

-9-

THICKENER

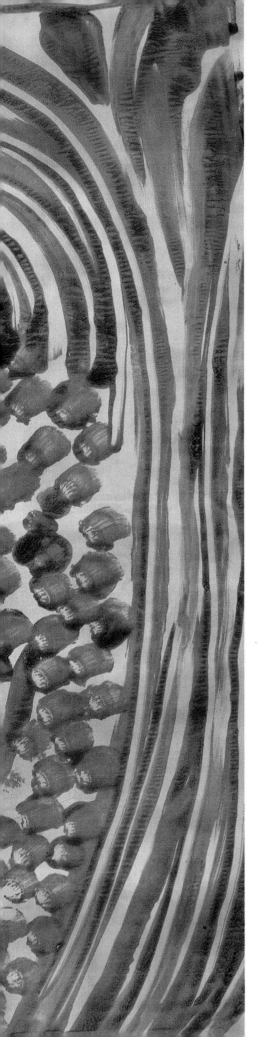

Thickener is a colourless gel used to thicken silk-painting dyes. It is also sometimes known as *épaissisant*. When this is added to the dyes, it is possible to paint directly on to the silk without the dye spreading. It is good for fine, detailed work. The thickened dye does not run through the silk, so you can paint directly on to even the very fine, lightweight silks without needing a gutta or wax outline to resist the spread of the dye, or having to coat the fabric with an anti-spread.

Thickened dye can also be used for a great variety of techniques: sponging, rolling, monoprinting, blockprinting, stencilling and screen-printing can all be carried out on silk once the dye has been thickened.

EQUIPMENT NEEDED

- Silk
- Thickener (*épaissisant*)
- Frame and pins
- Masking tape
- Dyes and brushes
- Sheet of glass
- Rollers
- Sponges
- Vegetables
- Printing block
- Card

Monoprint created by painting directly on to a sheet of glass with a brush (*see pages 90–1*)

THICKENER

Thickener is a water-based acrylic polymer product. It is non-toxic. Manufacturers have their own thickeners, so it may be a good idea to use the same make of thickener as the silk paint you are using, as the manufacturers suggest, although we have found that this does not really matter. Some thickeners come in powder form.

The thickener can be added to the dye in any proportion you like. To mix, just spoon some thickener into a dish and add some dye, stir well and it is ready to use. The thickness of the paste will depend on the technique you intend to use. A fairly thick, cream-like consistency is needed for screenprinting. If stencilling is your chosen technique, however, you will need to mix the dye paste a little thicker. If you are monoprinting, the paste should not be too thick or it will not spread easily on the glass.

SILK

All silks, both heavy and light-weight, are ideal for use with thickened dyes. If the silk chosen is a pongée 5 the dye will have to be thicker so that it does not spread. You will find if you are using a heavy crêpe de Chine or wild silk that not much thickener is needed to allow direct painting. Always experiment and paint a trial piece of silk first.

DYES

Different dye brands have their own thickeners. Opaque dyes do not spread quite so easily and will not

83

need to be thickened as much as thinner, transparent dyes. For all the following techniques the silk can be stretched over a frame, although for roller printing and blockprinting it is easier to stretch the fabric on the work surface over a padded, absorbent base. A sheet of felt or thin wadding covered in kraft paper or old sheeting can be used: the silk is stretched over this and attached with tape.

Repeat patterns painted directly on to the silk with a thickened dye

---

PAINTING DIRECT

Painting directly on to the silk with thickened dyes provides great freedom. The design can be as big as required; limited only by the size of your piece of silk (you could always sew several pieces of silk together, too) very large areas can be covered with big brushes and interesting textures can be created by brushstrokes.

Painting directly on to the silk is as simple as it sounds – just paint straight on to the silk. If the dye spreads too far you have not put enough thickener in it. You may paint whatever you desire in as many colours as you wish. Very fine,

detailed work is possible using a small sable brush. Try painting a watercolour background first with unthickened paints. Wait for it to dry before painting your motif or design with thickened dye. A large, one-off design can be painted, or a repeat pattern as shown in the photograph below.

When painting direct, if dry brushstrokes and textures are required with sharp, defined edges, you must let one colour dry thoroughly before applying the next. If a more watery effect is required, where the dyes merge and blend, work on wet or damp silk.

It is quite difficult to obtain very large plain areas by painting direct

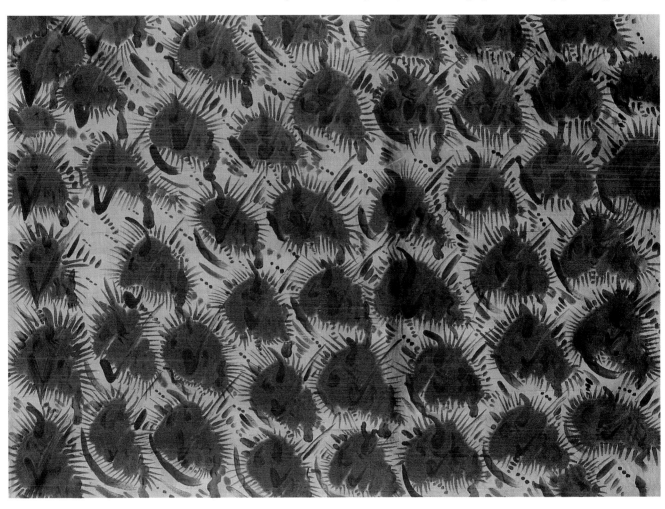

Brush prints. From top to bottom:
  silk-painting brush
  fan-shaped brush
  bristle brush dragged across the silk

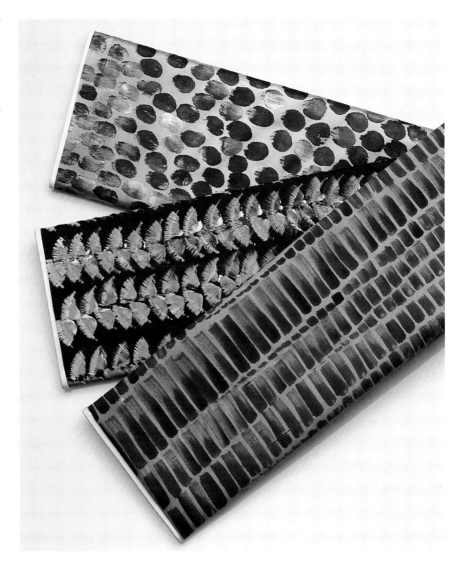

with thickened dyes, as they are difficult to spread evenly. The actual brushstroke may show, but this often produces a striking texture. You must be very careful with this approach, however, as the result can also turn out to look an absolute mess!

PRINTING WITH BRUSHES

Brushes of all shapes and sizes can also be used to print on silk. There are many shapes of brush available: pointed, square, round, fan and wedge. You can also cut your own shaped brushes. To print with a brush, dip it into the dish of thickened paste, scrape off the excess and print on to the silk. You can also try rolling and twisting the brush on the silk, or dragging it across in different directions. The speed of the brushstroke, the angle at which it is held and the quantity of paint on the brush will all affect the texture produced.

CARD PRINTING

A variety of objects can be used for printing: wood, metal, plastic, cork, various plants and natural objects. Card is quick and versatile. Corrugated card, ends of matchboxes, cardboard tubes, etc. can all be used. To print using card, dip the card into the thickened paint or paint the dye evenly on to the edge of the card. Print on to the silk.

(Below) Card print

After a while the edge of the card may become soggy and misshapen. If this happens, discard it and cut a new piece.

FRUIT AND VEGETABLE PRINTING

Many interesting textures and effects can be achieved by printing on to the silk with a variety of fruit and vegetables, and it is one of the simplest forms of printing. This method is very useful when a motif or design is wanted in a repeat

Fruit and vegetable prints

pattern, such as spots or stars, and it is very quick and easy.

You need a flat, even surface. Cut the fruit or vegetable in half with a large knife. If you are using a potato, you can cut a shape or design out of the flat surface using a small knife. Dab off the excess moisture and let it dry for about half an hour. Cover the flat side of the fruit or vegetable with a thin layer of paint (if you use too much, a thick, uneven edge will be produced when printed) and stamp it on to the silk.

You can also paint the fruit or vegetable each time by hand. If you do this you can apply two or three colours, but it is quicker to dip into a dye pad. Try covering a few paper towels in the dye paste and then stamping on to the silk – it makes for an even covering. If you find it difficult to keep hold of the fruit or vegetable, put a fork into it.

Block prints and wooden blocks

BLOCKPRINTING

Wood blocks and lino cuts can also be used with thickened dye paste. The paste is applied to the surface of the wood block or lino cut, which is then stamped on to the silk to make a print.

To coat the wood block evenly with dye paste, it is a good idea to use a roller and a sheet of glass. Roll the thickened dye out evenly on to the glass and then coat the wood block by rolling over it with the dye-covered roller. You can also paint the wood block with a brush: the advantage of this is that several colours can be painted on to the block exactly where you want them. You can also put several colours on the glass and roll the dye on to the block.

When the block is evenly coated with the thickened dye it can be

87

printed on the silk. Remember to do a trial print on a sample piece first.

SPONGING

Sponges are ideal for printing on silk and some super mottled textures can be achieved. Different types of sponges will produce different effects.

Cheap foam sponges and the more expensive natural sponges are easy to find and will produce good textures. The different textures obtained will depend entirely on whether the silk is wet or dry, the texture of the sponge, how much dye you let the sponge soak up and how hard you press the sponge on to the silk. The thicker dye paste works well with this technique as, if the paint is too thin, it will run and spread, losing its sponge-like texture.

To sponge on silk, stretch the silk flat on an absorbent pad. Prepare all the colours required, a dish for each colour. Dip the sponge into the paste and test first on a sample piece. Press the sponge on to the silk (not too heavily). When using two or more colours, remember that further colours will be created where they overlap. The dye pastes do dry out fairly quickly, so if you plan to sponge on large areas, spoon a little at a time on to the flat dish.

It is fun to experiment with this technique. You can mask out areas that do not require colour with masking tape or stencils. Try cutting your own shapes from big bath sponges or kitchen scourers.

Sponge prints and sponges

ROLLER PRINTING

Stretch the silk over a padded base. Put some thickened dye on a sheet of glass and roll it smooth all over the roller. Then roll the roller across the silk in any direction you require. Different colours may be rolled over each other in different directions. You can also use the roller to print shapes on to the silk or twist it as you print.

Unthickened silk paints can be used with sponge rollers, but with wooden and plastic rollers the dye must be thickened or it will not adhere to the roller.

MONOPRINTING

A monoprint is a one-off design which cannot be repeated. You will need a sheet of glass, the size of which will determine the size of your print.

Brush, sponge or roll a layer of thickened dye on to the glass. Then, using your finger, a stick, the end of a brush, a knitting needle or a roller, press hard into the dye, making marks in the paste rather like finger-painting. Try making swirling patterns with a roller or comb.

Immediately, before the paste has time to dry, place the silk on top of the design you have made. The image will always be printed in reverse, so if you want to write names or numbers remember to do so in mirror writing. If you are working on a very large piece of silk and find it difficult to place it over the glass, try stretching the silk on a frame and lowering this on to the dye-covered glass.

It is difficult to see in advance exactly how the finished piece will

---

Roller prints

Monoprint and equipment

look. If the dye paste is too thick when printed, it will smudge and the design will be blurred. If the paint is too thin, you will find that it dries before you have taken the print. Sometimes you can take two or three prints from one design, although of course the print will get lighter. Often the second print is better than the first one.

This technique has endless possibilities. Try rolling the glass with dye paste and placing some pressed flowers or grasses on to the dye before taking a print. Try using a comb, and wiggle, squiggle, sweep and curl. Make long, flowing waves and short dashes, dots and cross-hatching.

The piece shown on pages 82–3 was painted extremely quickly with dye paste directly on to glass. A print was made on pale grey silk, and some wonderful brushstroke textures can be seen.

Many varied and interesting textures can be printed in this manner and they can be especially useful for patchwork and appliqué.

TIPS

- Make sure that fruit and vegetables are dry before putting dye on them.
- Always paint or print a trial piece to ascertain how far the dye will spread.
- Work quickly when attempting a monoprint or the dye paste will dry.
- When using sheet glass, bind the edges with masking tape to prevent accidents.

-10-
CRAYONS

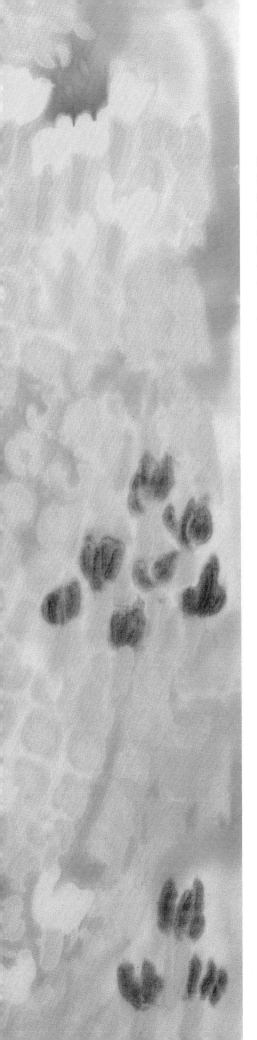

Fabric crayons are becoming increasingly popular with adults and children alike. They are widely available in craft and fabric shops, and may be used on silk and many other fabrics. Whilst being attractive on their own, you can produce more subtle results by combining them with silk paints in mixed-media work.

There are two types of crayons on the market: steam-fixed and iron-fixed. Steam-fixed crayons may be used as a resist with dyes as well as on their own. When the crayon is melted into the fabric using a hairdryer, the wax barrier forms an outline which can be painted around. Iron-fixed crayons do not spread in this way, so they do not create an effective barrier, although this does not mean that they cannot be used with dyes. Painting the silk with background colours and highlighting with crayons can be attractive.

EQUIPMENT NEEDED

- Silk
- Crayons: iron-fixed and steam-fixed
- Hairdryer
- Iron
- Paper
- Protective cloth
- Dyes
- Frame and pins
- Brushes
- Masking tape

Spring garden. Created with steam-fixed crayons (*see overleaf*)

SILK

All types of silk may be used for this technique. The crayons, when used lightly, will tend to colour only the surface of the fabric: bold colours will need firmer application of the crayons. Thicker silks may not allow the crayons to penetrate through. Care must be taken using steam-fixed crayons with thick silk, as, when melted with a hairdryer, the crayons may not create a sufficiently strong barrier for the dyes.

The surface texture of the silk can in itself be of interest with crayons. A slubbed wild silk or bourette produces unusual textures when crayoned.

PREPARING THE SILK

The crayons are made up of wax and pigment, and resemble children's wax crayons. They can be used in a similar way, drawing on to the surface of the silk instead of on to paper.

The silk needs to be stretched for easy crayoning. The simplest way is to attach the silk with masking tape to a flat surface such as a light-coloured melamine table. An alternative is to stretch the silk on to a silk-painting frame so that the silk is in firm contact with the table. The design and crayoning are therefore carried out on the underside of the silk. Movement of the work is much simpler if this method is used, making the drying of dyes and crayons with the hairdryer easier.

The design can either be drawn directly on to the silk using a marker pen and pencil, or can be traced through the silk from the surface beneath.

IRON-FIXED CRAYONS

Brilliant basic colours are available from several manufacturers (see the list of suppliers on pages 123–5). Their colours stand out well against light-coloured backgrounds.

The crayons become permanent in the fabric when ironed. Place a sheet of paper over the surface of the crayon and iron thoroughly (you may wish to cover the ironing-board to prevent crayons printing through). The work is now washable.

When using these crayons with a steam-fixed dye, iron the crayons into the fabric first, before steaming the dyes.

STEAM-FIXED CRAYONS

These look similar to the iron-fixed crayons, so be sure to read the manufacturer's instructions very carefully to ascertain which type you have.

We have found that these crayons tend to be softer than the iron-fixed type and become rather sticky when held for any length of time. The crayons melt easily when heated by a hand-held hairdryer.

The silk is stretched and crayoned in a similar way to the iron-fixed crayons. Ensure that any gaps in the design are filled in, or the dye will leak through when painted later on. Heat the silk evenly with a hairdryer until all the wax has melted. Allow the silk to cool.

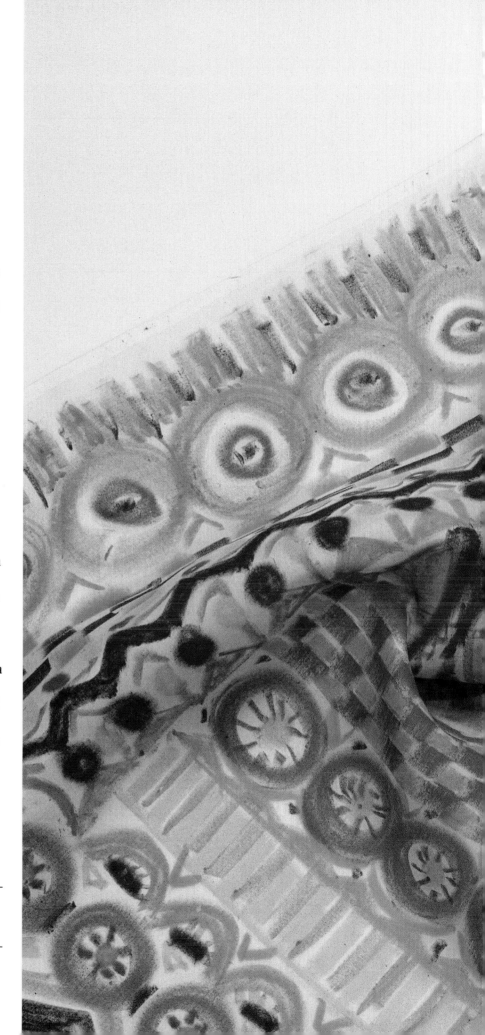

Bright geometric patterns made with iron-fixed crayons

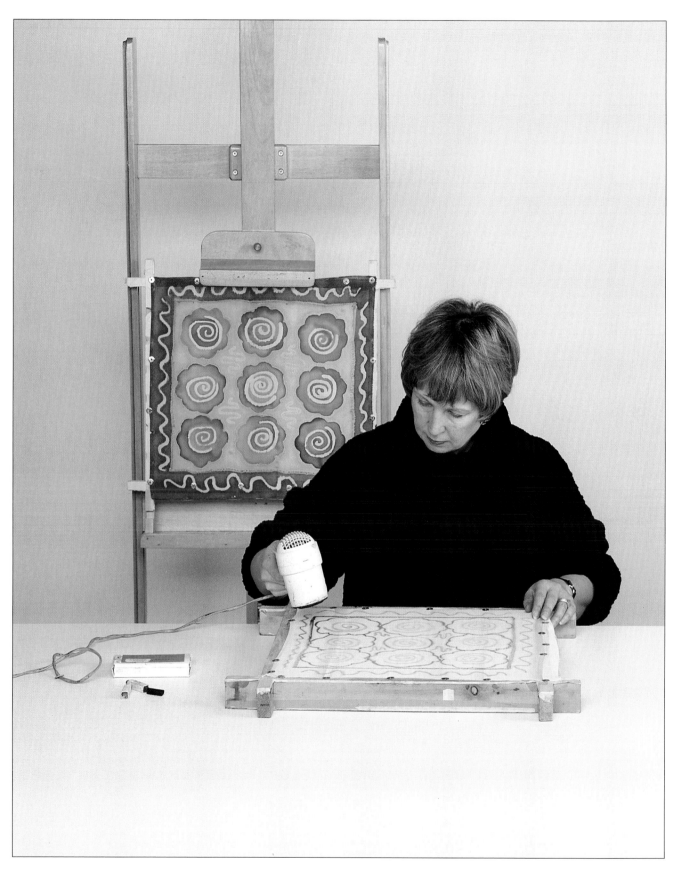

Various items rubbed for their textures

The work is then ready to paint. Take care not to overload the surface of the silk with dye, or the barriers may not hold, and try not to paint over the crayon because some of the dye outline will be spoiled. The resisting edges of the crayon are often encroached on by the dyes, but the textured effect that results is often interesting.

Melting wax crayons to form a resist before painting on the dyes

When steaming the silk (see pages 119–21), remember to place a double piece of paper over the work to prevent reprinting on the silk.

METHODS OF CREATING TEXTURES WITH CRAYONS

Rubbing

Anything with a distinct surface texture can be used. Natural forms such as bark, leaves, grass and grit and man-made articles such as graters, plastic lids, string, doilies, lace and nets are all suitable.

Place the items on a flat surface (they may need to be taped into place or even pinned to stop them moving around). Lay the fabric on top and gently rub across the objects with the crayons, with your free hand holding the silk steady. Try not to smudge the crayons as you work. Try stretching your silk on to a silk-painting frame before placing over the textures; this may help to keep the items and silk steady as you crayon.

Rubbings can be built up into textural pictures, which can be enhanced with free crayoning.

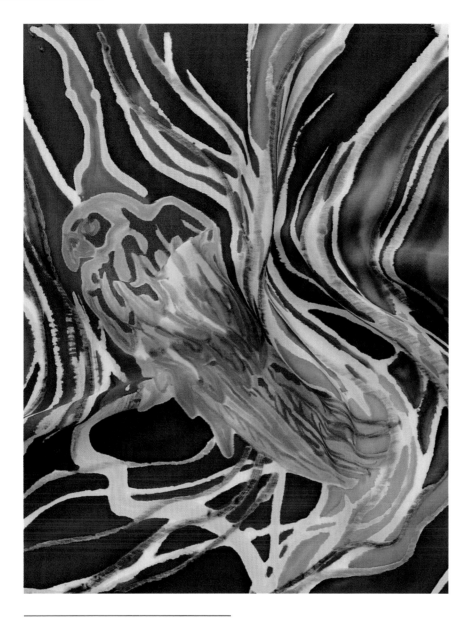

Parrot. Created with melted steam-fixed crayons, showing resisting qualities and textures

Grating

Strong blobs of colour can be melted into the fabric. Iron over waxed paper to spread the blobs over the surface of the silk. Grate directly on to the silk.

Patterning

Use the crayons to mark the fabric. Experiment with stippling, rolling, twisting and scoring to create different intensities of colour.

Samples showing the use of iron-fixed crayons

Printing

Leaves or coarse-textured cloths are ideal for this method. Gently rub the crayons over the veined backs of the leaves or over the rough surface of the cloth. Place these items in the desired position and cover with greaseproof paper. Iron carefully over the paper until the wax crayons have printed on to the silk and melted into the fabric.

TIPS

- Vary the weight of crayoning to alter the texture.
- Remember that steam-fixed dyes spread when heated with the hairdryer. Delicate, intricate patterns cannot be created with this technique.
- Colour the backgrounds with dye after crayoning. The textures of the encroaching dye are interesting.
- Keep the crayons cool or they will melt and snap easily.

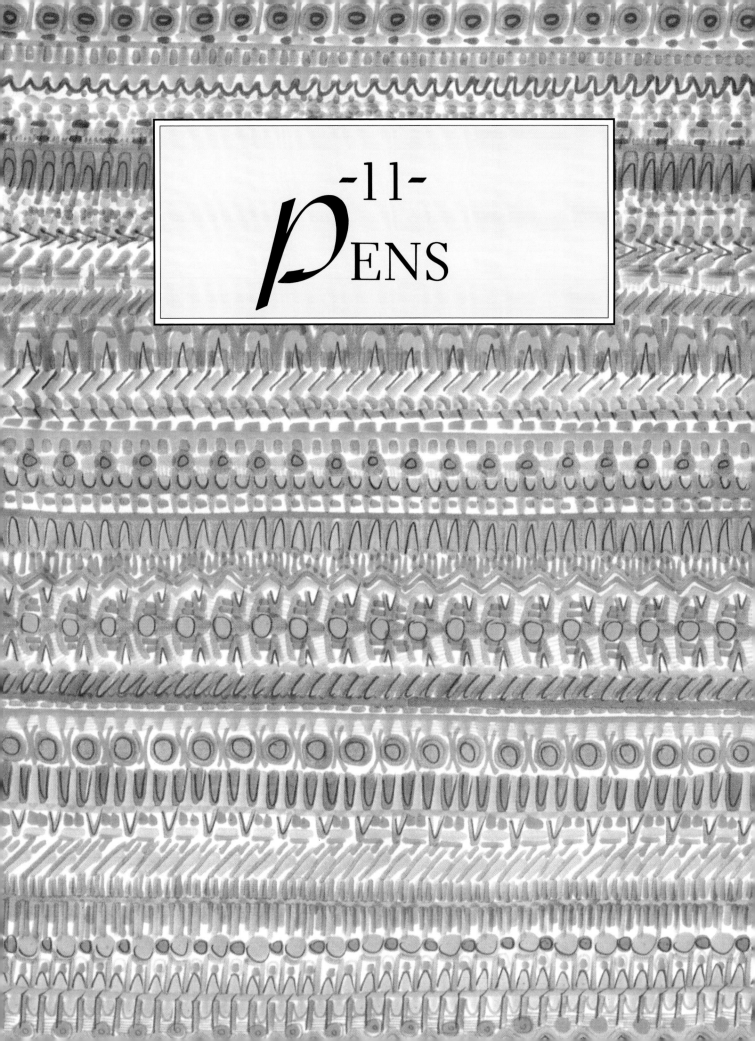

-11-

PENS

Fabric pens which look and work like ordinary felt-tip pens are now made especially for use on fabrics. They are very easy to control and ideal for children as they are non-toxic and no mess is involved. They are useful for a wide range of activities, especially linear work and intricate patterns, but they will not show up on dark-coloured silk.

Permanent markers can also enhance your silk painting. They are not made especially for silk painting, but they are permanent and they do enable very fine line drawing. They are also good for signing your work.

A wide variety of glitter, metallic, coloured, fluorescent and pearlized outliners are now available. These can be bought in bottles and tubes and are all for surface decoration. They are very useful as they *do* show up on dark-coloured silks. Most are now available in art and craft shops.

EQUIPMENT NEEDED

- Silk
- Fabric pens
- Permanent markers
- Glitter, metallic, coloured, fluorescent and pearlized outliners
- Dyes and brushes
- Frame and pins

(Previous page)
Detailed fabric-pen design on pongée 9

SILK

These pens and markers can be used on all silks, but if you are using a very fine silk be prepared for them to spread a little. You could always put on a thin coat of anti-spread to ensure no spread at all.

DYES

If you wish to colour your silk before using the pens and markers, paint with your usual dyes first and fix in the usual way.

FABRIC PENS

Fabric pens are dye-filled felt-tip pens. They come in several sizes: thin, medium and some lovely big fat ones. They are not suitable for very dark-coloured silk as they will not show up. The thin pens are excellent for detailed linear work, intricate patterns and small details. They are not quite as bright as silk paints, but you can put on two or three coats if needed.

Fabric pens are fade-resistant and machine-washable, once they have been fixed. They are fixed into the silk by ironing on the reverse side with a hot iron. Some brands of fabric pen are refillable and new fibre tips can be bought. The colour range is somewhat limiting, but you can over-paint and create new colours.

PERMANENT MARKERS

Permanent markers are very useful. We always keep several black ones and various sizes of gold and silver in the studio. The fine and superfine black markers are useful for very fine

details and outlining. Try drawing or outlining over already-painted silk to create more definition and emphasize certain areas and shapes. Permanent markers are toxic, so be careful if children are handling them. The fine black markers are useful for signing your work and the gold and silver ones are very effective when used on dark-coloured silks. The silk may be washed in lukewarm soapy water.

OUTLINERS

There are now many brands of liners available for fabric painting, and most of these can be used on silk. Check the manufacturer's instructions. The puffa or heat-expanding paints are not recommended for silk, although we have found them serviceable on heavier silks (fine silks pucker).

These liners come in tubes or bottles and you will find many different varieties: glitter, metallic, coloured, fluorescent and pearlized. They are called 'surface-decoration' pens as this is literally what they do. A raised line which looks like wet plastic forms on the silk, sometimes called liquid embroidery. Outliners are great fun to use on their own, or in conjunction with your hand-painted silks. They are very effective on both light- and dark-coloured silks. Try the gold and silver glitter on black silk. Children will love the pearlized and fluorescent liners.

TECHNIQUES

All these dye pens and markers can be drawn directly on to the silk. This can be done by stretching the silk

Squares and rectangles using thick felt-tip marker pens

out on to a flat surface or on a frame. Remember to put some paper underneath if you are working on a flat surface, or your design will be repeated all over the table! Try using the fabric pens on silk that you have already painted, making sure that the silk has been fixed first.

Large pens are ideal for doodles, scribbles and wild designs, while thin pens enable you to create intricate designs and complicated patterns. When drawing, try not to go too slowly or the dye may spread

Gold and silver marker pens

Drawing patterns with felt-tip pens

too far across the silk (a hairdryer can be used to stop dyes spreading). The fabric pens are fixed by ironing on the wrong side with a hot iron. Try using your pens on a wet background for a softer, diffused look.

Permanent markers can be used on your work before or after fixing the silk if it has already been painted. The ink comes out of the nib by pumping the tip up and down, so try this on a piece of paper before drawing on your silk. These pens are fixed using a hot iron. If, however, you have combined them

(*Below*)
Felt-tip pens on a wet, painted background

Pearlized and glitter outliners

IRON-ON PENS

These pens enable you to transfer your design on to the silk. First, draw the motif or pattern on to tracing paper, then trace over the outlines of the design on the reverse side with the iron-on pen. Turn the design over and place it on the silk. Setting the iron to the silk setting, iron on the design.

There are also pens which will allow the design to print more than once if a repeat motif is required. The pen lines do not vanish as with the fabric marker pen, but they can be washed out.

with dyes which need steam-fixing, make sure you put two or three layers of paper over them as they tend to reprint.

Glitter, pearlized, fluorescent and coloured outliners can be used on silk that has been stretched flat on a work surface or stretched on to a frame. Most outliners are washable at 60°C. Some are even boilable, so be sure to read the instructions on the tube on aftercare. Some require fixing with a hot iron or hairdryer; others do not require any fixing at all. The liners sit on the surface of the silk, so, when painted, the silk will have a very definite right and wrong side.

FABRIC MARKER PENS

These pens are very useful for drawing your design on to the silk at the beginning of your project. Unless you are a very accomplished artist and can draw freehand, you will want an outline from which to work. Place your drawing under the silk and trace it on to the silk using the fabric marker pen.

These pens look like felt-tip pens, but the purple line vanishes after several hours. There is also a pen which makes a line that vanishes in water; this is very useful for drawing your designs on silk instead of using a pencil.

TIPS

● Fix painted silk before drawing on it with fabric pens.
● Use two or three layers of fixing paper if you have used permanent markers.
● Do not draw too slowly with the pens.
● Do not try to cover very large areas with the pens.
● If very fine, even lines are required when using a glitter pen, try attaching a nomographic nib. Use nos. 7–9, as anything finer will become blocked very easily.

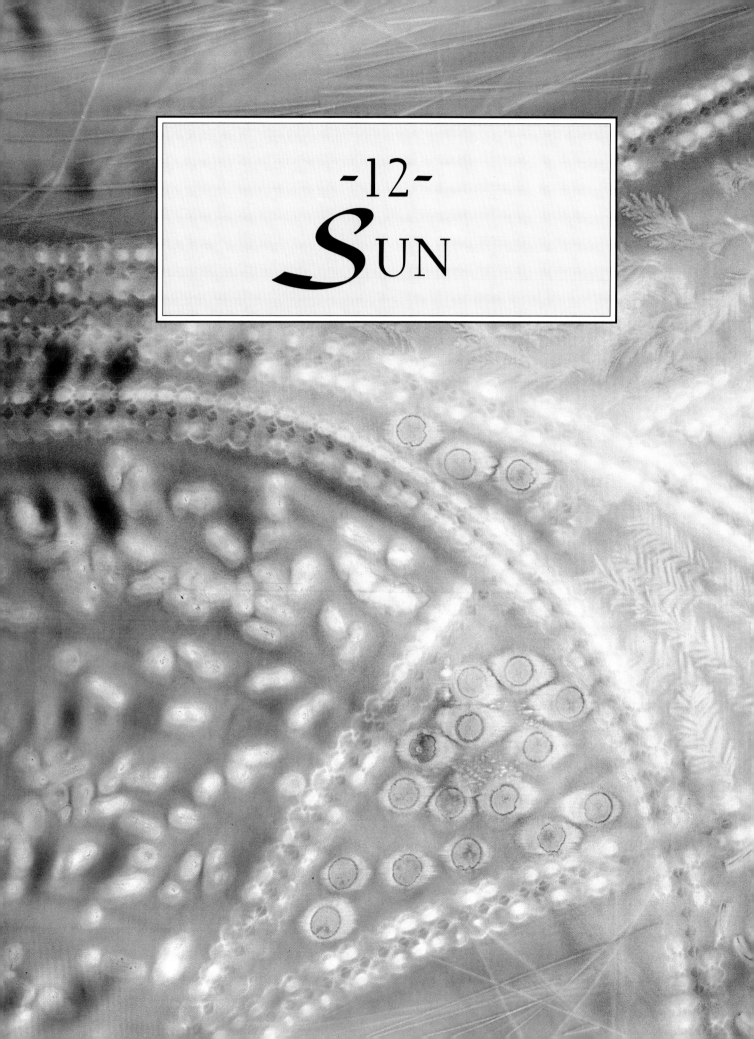

-12-
Sun

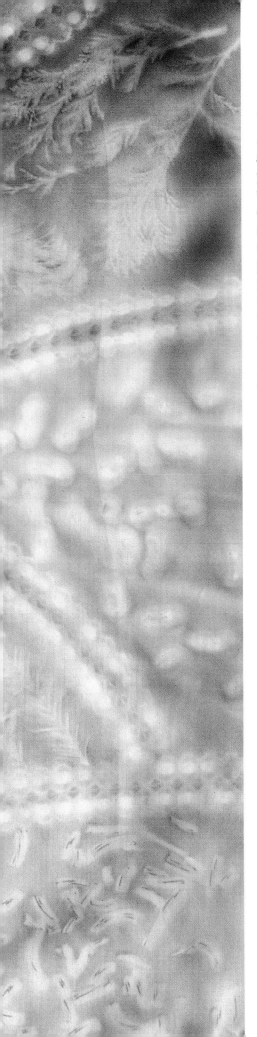

Paint a piece of silk with a wash of dye and lay it in the sunshine, and what do you have? A piece of painted silk. Paint a piece of silk with a wash of setacolor transparent dye, place some leaves on the surface and lay it in the sun, and what do you have? A piece of painted silk with incredible leaf prints all over the surface. These dyes react with light to give super textured effects with very little effort on your part.

EQUIPMENT NEEDED

- Silk
- Setacolor transparent dyes
- Found, natural objects
- Templates
- Light source: sun, halogen lamp, sun lamp or infra-red lamp
- Brushes
- Paper or card
- Scissors

Setacolor transparent dyes and their unusual properties are used in the sunshine of Pacific islands for decorating pareos and sarongs for summer beachwear. We too can decorate silk with pretty patterns in this way. Sunlight reacts with the dyes, but you can create the effect indoors using strong lamps.

Pasta and lace on satin

CREATING A REACTION WITH DYES

Stretch the silk on to a frame and dampen the surface using a large brush and water. Dilute the dyes with water (one volume of dye and up to two volumes of water depending on the strength of colour you require). Paint the surface of the silk, then place on the wet silk either a template or some objects which will resist the light. Place the frame outside in strong sunshine or inside under strong lamps. The lamps should provide a total of at least 240 watts to create the strength needed for a reaction: you will need to experiment for yourself with the lighting you have available. Try to have the light source pointing at the silk from above, rather than from the side, or you may find that the reaction will not be as great in areas further away from the light.

Allow the silk to dry naturally. Do not disturb the frame at all or you could accidentally blur the results. When the silk is dry, remove the objects. The light will have reacted with the dye: the areas of silk under the templates or objects will be light in colour, with their outer edges sharply defined against the stronger background colour.

SILK

Any type of silk may be used for this technique. We have found that the use of a fine silk such as crêpe georgette results in a soft, subtle reaction to the light. The shiny surface of satin seems to accentuate and enhance the technique; the photograph on the left shows a lovely example of this.

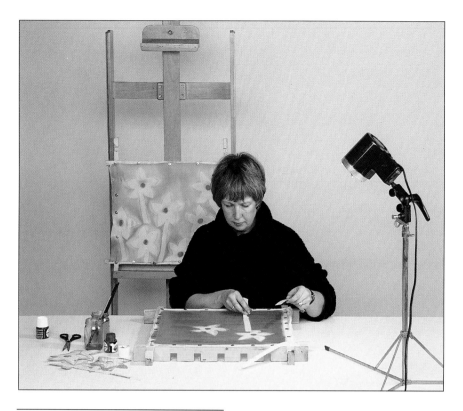

Daffodils. Templates being used to resist the light

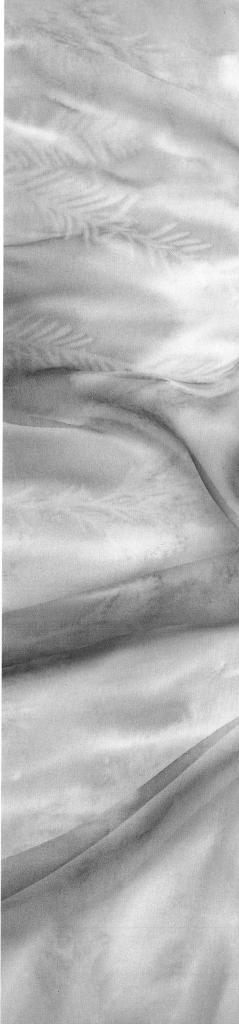

BLOCKING THE LIGHT

The effect of this technique is created by blocking the light with objects placed on the silk. Anything can be used; either natural or man-made. If you use natural items such as leaves, ferns or houseplants, make sure that they will not shrivel during exposure to the lamps or sunlight. Evergreens such as yew, conifer and laurel leaves are ideal. Older fern leaves are successful too, as well as waxy, broad-leaved houseplants. They can be placed at random over the surface or cut and carefully placed to produce stylized patterns. The more definite the edge of the leaves, the more effective the shape produced will be.

Feathers will also be effective, especially if they are large and flat. Peacock feathers on a blue-green wash would be very interesting, for example.

All sorts of cooking ingredients can be used for this technique, including a whole range of pasta shapes. If these are organized in blocks they will create different textures.

Fine crêpe-georgette silk with yew-tree-leaf resists

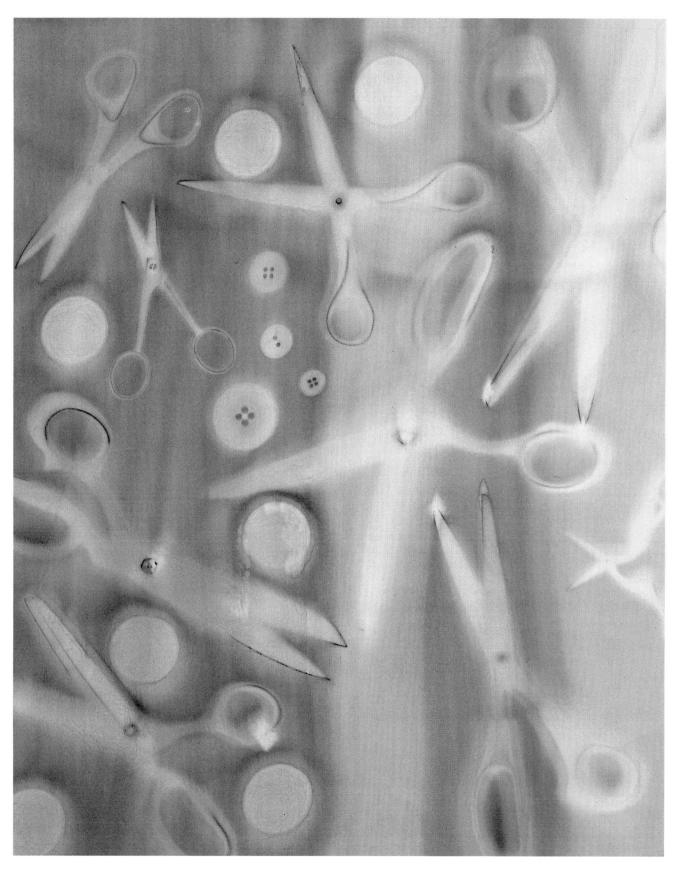

that you are placing on the silk. The reverse idea could be tried by using a stencil. The light will only shine on to the cut-out spaces to form a pattern.

FIXING

Setacolor transparent dyes are fixed into the silk, when dry, with a hot iron. Place a cloth over the painted silk and iron carefully for up to two minutes. The silk will then be washable and dry-cleanable. See pages 118–21 for further information on fixing methods.

Man-made materials, such as metal grills, grids, lattice-work or woven fabrics, including lace, net, scrim or distorted hessian, are also effective. In these two examples we have used easily distinguishable objects such as a variety of scissors, buttons and tennis racquets.

Scissors and buttons – 'found' objects

HOME-MADE RESISTS

Try making your own templates to resist the light. Using pinking shears, which create an attractive edge, cut out strips of stiff card and overlap them to give a geometric design. Cut out simple flower shapes: lilies, daffodils and roses all have easily recognizable outlines. You could perhaps paint the area beneath the template a different tone or colour, to emphasize the shape

TIPS

● Do *not* move the frame during the course of drying, or you may blur the results.
● Choose objects which have a definite outline.
● Check that leaves are dry and clean, or they will mark the silk.

111

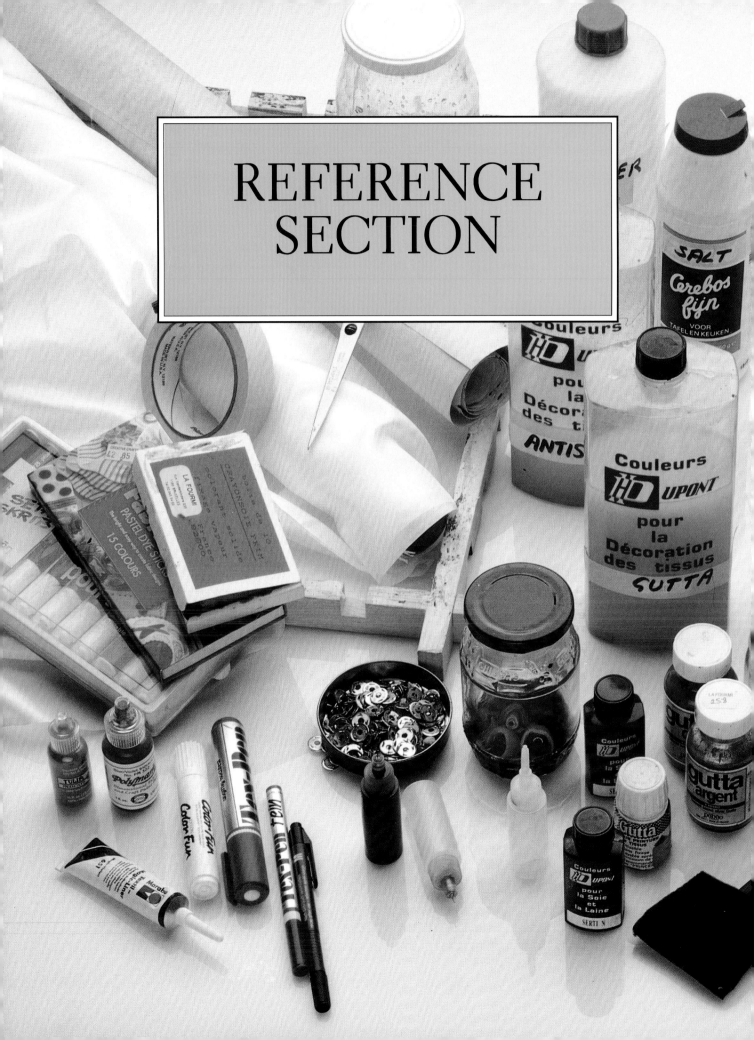

REFERENCE SECTION

The techniques described in this book are extensive, and each one requires specific equipment to achieve the different textures. The details of the equipment needed are given in each chapter, and so this is a general outline of the basic elements. Some of the equipment is common to all the techniques and is dealt with in the following pages.

THE WORKPLACE

Some of the techniques included in the book are extremely messy. You may be lucky enough to have a room in your home which can be specifically kept for silk painting, and where you can leave unfinished work undisturbed. Alternatively, a garage or a shed could be used, in which case the need for protecting the walls and floor would be lessened. Otherwise it is important to cover furniture and carpets with sheets of polythene or newspaper. Even unfixed dyes sometimes cannot be removed, however hard you try, so care is needed. Remember that when spraying with an aerosol canister a fine mist of dye can carry a long way in the air and will settle on every surface.

Working outside is ideal in the spring and summer months, although if it is too hot the sun will dry the dyes very quickly, which does not suit every technique (particularly salt). Spraying and dripping would be better performed outside, but beware of windy days when spraying.

(Previous page)
Basic silk-painting equipment

Good lighting is important in the workroom. Remember that artificial light alters colour tones tremendously. Light bulbs are now available which simulate a 'natural' daylight effect. Try to use these wherever possible.

Ventilation of the room is also important when you are using alcohol, methanol, white spirit or wax, and a small face mask is advisable if you will be spraying with an aerosol canister, as you should not inhale particles of dye.

The availability of a sink for changing water and cleaning dye baths and equipment is helpful. It is not a good idea to carry dyes over unprotected carpeted areas. Before you start to paint, consider all that you are going to have to do during the project and gather together all the necessary equipment in an accessible place.

Work is normally carried out on a light-coloured, flat, stable surface. A good-sized table should do, but if you are working with long frames and substantial lengths of fabric, you may need a trestle table (this can be packed away when not in use). Try to set up your table with room for movement all around it, so that painting can be relaxed without you having to move furniture out of the way at a crucial point.

Once your workroom is protected and prepared, check that you have removed any jewellery or loose sleeves which could drag in your work. Always wear old clothes and an apron or shirt for protection. Wear surgical gloves if your hands will come into contact with a lot of dye during the course of painting or dripping the silk. A new hand-cleaning paste is now available; it is also useful for clothing when spots of dye have marked a garment. It is very strong and should be used with caution on coloured fabrics.

MATERIALS AND EQUIPMENT

Silk

Silk is a beautiful fabric and, when painted, the colours of the dyes reflect its natural lustre and gloss. The fabric is unique in its characteristics: it has considerable strength, and yet is fine and supple to the touch. It is warm in winter and yet cool to wear in the summer.

As with other fabrics, silk can be woven in various ways to produce fabrics of different weights and textures. The more expensive silks are of a better weight and composition. When embarking on a new piece of work it is very important to choose the correct silk. Consideration must be given to the final use of the silk, whether it be for clothes, scarves or interior-upholstery purposes. This is a vital decision as the finished project needs to be serviceable.

The second consideration is the technique that is to be used on the silk, as the results will often depend on its texture and weight. A fine, delicate antifusant picture could not be created as easily on a wild silk as on a pongée, for example. The slubs in the wild silk would resist the even painting necessary for detailed work, whereas pongée is a fine, evenweave silk.

The chart opposite shows some examples of readily-available silks which can be used for your projects.

Fabric	Description	Use	Technique
Chiffon	Sheer, lightweight, transparent plainweave. Usually soft but sometimes with stiff finish.	Scarves, sheer blouses, eveningwear, window drapes, bedroom cushions.	Watercolour, sugar, salt, alcohol, wax, spray, gutta, sun.
Crêpe de Chine	Lustrous plainweave silk. Light, medium or heavyweight. Drapes beautifully and is lovely to work on.	Underwear, nightwear, clothes, scarves, cushions, wallhangings, lampshades, accessories.	All techniques.
Crêpe georgette	Sheer, textured crêpe fabric with crinkly surface. Heavier than chiffon.	Scarves, eveningwear, hair accessories, window drapes.	Watercolour, sugar, salt, alcohol, wax, spray, gutta, sun.
Pongée (Habutai, Japanese silk)	Shiny, evenweave silk, often sold as jacket-lining silk. Weights from 05-014. The higher the number, the thicker and stronger the silk. Ideal for silk painting. Reasonable price.	Clothes, scarves, cushions, lampshades, pictures, wallhangings. This is the most useful of the silk fabrics.	All techniques.
Satin	Smooth silk with a high sheen. Often seen in a patterned jacquard weave. Luxurious feel.	Underwear, nightwear, blouses, jackets, belts, bedroom accessories.	All techniques.
Twill	A strong silk with a definite diagonal weave in light, medium and heavy weights.	Scarves (men and women), ties, cummerbunds, cushions, pictures.	All techniques.
Taffeta	Finely woven fabric. Has a crisp papery feel. Expensive.	Evening dresses, skirts, jackets, ties or bow-ties, cummerbunds, cushions.	All techniques. *Some movement of salt.*
Dupion (wild silk, *soie sauvage*)	Silk with an uneven texture or 'slubs'. Fairly stiff to handle.	Eveningwear. Excellent for ties and bow-ties. Also for cushions and home furnishings requiring a thicker fabric.	All techniques. Excellent for thickened dyes. *Some movement of salt.*

The samples overleaf show the reaction of a water-based dye on different silks. Each colour dot varies according to the construction, thickness and type of silk. The results are useful for deciding on the method of painting. In some cases the dye spreads quickly; in others there is little movement.

In order to make them feel heavier, some silks have a finish applied to their surface by the manufacturer. The silk should be washed by hand before painting if this is the case, although this is very seldom necessary (see notes on washing on page 121).

Frames

A wooden frame is essential for painting on silk, as the fabric has to be raised above the work surface. The silk can be stretched taut on many types of frames which are now widely available in art and craft shops.

The 'fixed' wooden frame is easily constructed using four pieces of soft wood cut to the required size. These can be glued or nailed together using butt or mitred joints (see illustration overleaf).

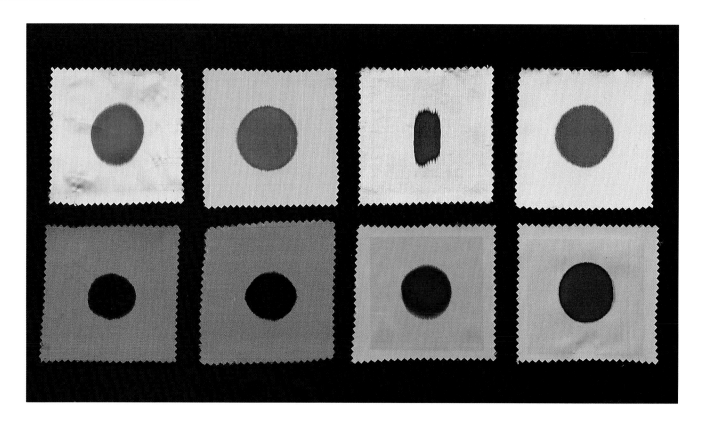

Silk dye-spots.
Top row, from left to right:
   twill
   satin
   wild silk
   tussah
Bottom row, from left to right:
   organza
   crêpe georgette
   crêpe de Chine
   pongée 9

More sophisticated frames can make finer adjustments, depending on the size of the silk on which you are working. The 'slot' frame and the 'sliding' frame (which uses screws and wing-nuts), are much more versatile. A soft-wood adjustable 'slot' frame, which accommodates a 90 × 90 cm (36 × 36 ins) piece of fabric, is most useful.

Smaller pieces of work could be stretched across a tambour embroidery hoop or a stiff cardboard box. Pre-stretched silks mounted on to fine metal frames are a recent innovation; these can only be used with iron- or hairdryer-fixed dyes.

Pins

Unless you have invested in a magnetic frame, or one with prongs mounted on to a strip, it will be necessary to hold the silk on the frame with three-pronged architect's pins. Push pins or ordinary tacks can be used if they have fine points, but they tend to tear the silk at the edges.

A new system of fine hooks, which are held on to frames with rubber bands, is useful for pre-hemmed scarves because it enables the silk to be painted right to the edges without pin-marks showing.

Stretching the silk

Before attaching the silk it is a good idea to protect the frame by covering the top surface with masking tape. Dye-stained tape can be removed after the completion of each project.

Stretch the silk, with the design side uppermost, tightly down one side of the frame, using the straight grain as a guide. Pin into place.

Adjustable 'slot' frame

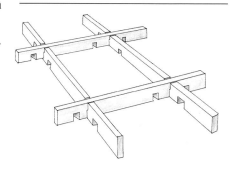

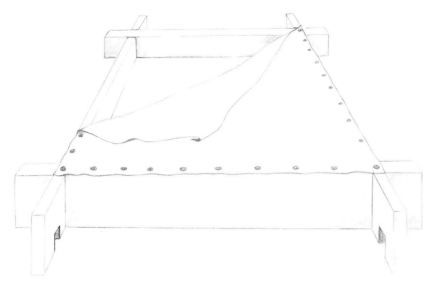

Silk stretched and pinned on to a 'slot' frame

Continue stretching and pinning the opposite side and then the remaining two sides. Make sure that the silk is as tight as a drum and that the design is not distorted (a design is usually drawn on prior to pinning so that any straight lines within it are accurate, as the pinning tends to pull them out of shape).

Dyes

The variety of dyes that can be used for silk painting has increased enormously, and they are now widely available from good art and craft shops and by mail order. The techniques in the book show the use of many types of dyes, from translucent steam-fixed dyes to heat-fixed felt-tip pens. Many more interesting textures and effects can be created by super-imposing one on another. We hope to awaken your creative ideas!

The range of dyes and paints may seem bewildering to a beginner, but they can be categorized depending on their method of fixing. At all times follow the manufacturer's instructions for fixing. Care must be taken if you are using products on the same piece of work which require different fixing methods. In this case, each must be dealt with after the dye has dried.

The dyes must be fixed permanently into the silk fabric, or the colours will run and mark if splashed, and will fade in strong sunlight.

Steam-fixed dyes
These are transparent and penetrate the fabric thoroughly. The depth of colour is increased after fixing, producing strong, permanent colour. The dyes are diluted with water, dilutant or alcohol. They are very economical to use.

Iron-fixed paints
These colours are technically paints, but they are so thin that they act like dyes. They do not spread as far as transparent dyes when painted on silk, and some techniques, such as watercolour, salt and alcohol, may

be less effective with heat-fixed than with steam-fixed dyes. The reverse of the fabric is also less vibrant than the top side. These paints are very easy to use because they can be fixed quickly using an iron or a hairdryer.

Attractive pearlized and fluorescent colours are now on the market. These can be watered down and used to great effect. Some wax crayons and textile marker pens, which are useful for children, are also available, and are fixed in the same way.

Liquid-fixed dyes
These are similar to steam-fixed dyes, but have an alternative method of fixing. They can also be steamed.

Procion dyes
These extremely strong dyes are used mainly by the professional painter, who can colour the fabric either by dipping it into a dye bath, or by painting direct. The ingredients require careful mixing, but the dyes need no fixing after painting.

Individual silk painters will decide which dye suits their personal requirements. Each chapter gives detailed instructions on the use of the dyes and their proportions of dilutant. Check the instructions carefully before you begin painting.

Painting equipment

The textures created with the different dyes vary, as does the choice of applicator. There are many of these available, from specialist silk-painting brushes to cotton wool, cotton buds, pipettes, rollers and sponges. Palettes and jars for storing water and dyes need to be readily available, as do spoons and droppers for certain techniques.

A general rule is to keep all your equipment clean and rinsed thoroughly. Brushes should be stored with their tips uppermost.

Drawing equipment

Magic marker pens, felt-tip pens, hard and soft pencils, a pencil sharpener, an eraser, plastic and metal rulers, white drawing paper, tracing paper, kitchen roll, newspaper and masking tape may all be used.

Miscellaneous equipment

A hairdryer, paper and fabric scissors, a Stanley knife and a cutting board will all be necessary items.

FIXING AND AFTERCARE

Silk paints and dyes need to be fixed permanently into the silk to allow it to be washed and to prevent it from fading in the sunlight. There are several ways in which this can be done, depending on the dyes used, and it is important to check the method of fixing when purchasing your dyes.

The fixing process sets the dye into the silk. If the dyes are not fixed, the colour will run when the item is washed, the colours will fade in the sun, and the painted silk will watermark and stain if it comes into contact with water. Silk which has not been fixed should therefore be kept in a dry, dark place to prevent accidental watermarking and fading. Transparent silk dyes must be fixed

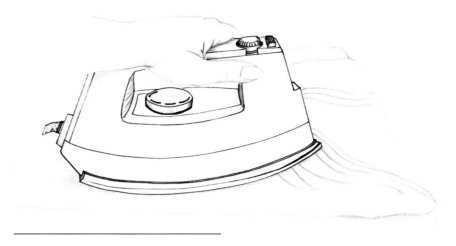

Fixing painted silk with an iron

into the silk by steaming or liquid-fixing; opaque silk paints are set with a hot iron or hairdryer.

Iron-fixing

This is the easiest method of fixing, and is used for silk paints. Wait until the silk is completely dry and then iron it with a hot, dry iron on the reverse side for about three minutes. Certain dyes can be fixed by using a hairdryer on the hot setting. This

Dipping silk into a bowl of liquid fixer

takes quite a long time and great care must be taken not to burn the silk, but on items such as lampshades or screens it may be necessary. The dyes are now permanent and can be washed in lukewarm water or dry-cleaned.

New brands of dye are coming on to the market and there are now some dyes which need no fixing at all – the silk is just left in the air.

Sometimes, when ironed, coloured and metallic guttas print on to your ironing-board. If the silk is then moved and ironed further, you may be in danger of gutta marks reprinting all over the silk and spoiling your work. Use some old, clean sheeting or kraft paper to protect the ironing-board, which may be adjusted if printing of gutta occurs.

Liquid-fixing

Some dyes are fixed using a silk-dye liquid-fixer. This makes silks lightfast, washable and dry-cleanable. Ensure that the silk is dry, and then coat or soak it in the liquid to cure for approximately one hour. (Some fixers have a longer fixing time than others, depending on the brand.) The silk is then rinsed in warm water to remove the fixer and any excess colour. Liquid-fixed dyes can also be fixed in a steamer. Beware that if you put water-based gutta in the liquid it will turn sticky.

Steam-fixing

Transparent silk dyes require steam for fixing. If you are only producing small amounts of painted silk, you can do your own steaming in a pressure cooker or send it to a steaming service (some of these are listed on page 126). If you are going to be producing large quantities, however, it would be wise to invest in a steamer.

Steamed colours are brilliant, vibrant and permanent. After the silk has been steam-fixed it is colourfast and can be washed and dry-cleaned. Steam-fixing does require special care, as the silk will be ruined if it is carried out incorrectly. If you do not trust yourself with a special length of silk which has just taken you hours to paint, send it to a steaming service or take it to your dry-cleaners: they sometimes have a steam-box in which they can steam your precious

work. Silk on which some water-soluble guttas have been used may turn gooey when steamed.

Pressure cooker

A pressure cooker is very useful for smaller pieces of work. Place each piece of silk flat on several layers of paper. Brown paper (with no wax coating), lining paper or kraft paper are all suitable, or you can buy large rolls of fixing paper. Do not use newspaper: the printing ink may reprint on the silk. Roll the silk and paper together, then flatten and seal the ends using tape which can withstand moisture. Tuck the ends in towards the centre, then roll and flatten again to form a small, firm package.

Fill the bottom of the pressure cooker with water to a depth of about 2 cm. Place the packages of silk in a basket on the trivet (when boiling, the water must not touch the packages). To prevent the packages getting wet from the condensation, cover them with paper. Finally, cover the whole basket with a large sheet of foil so that the condensation runs down into the water. Seal the lid and cook under pressure for 45 minutes.

Once the pressure cooker has cooled, carefully remove the lid, foil and paper. Remove the basket and take out the silk from the packages.

Steaming machines

Vertical steamer
The vertical steamer is a double-walled, stainless-steel cylinder. The tube rests on a container of water. Some steamers are fitted with an

element which makes steaming very easy, but the manual vertical steamer uses a gas ring or an electric hot-plate. The steamer is sealed at the top by a dome-shaped lid which has a hole in it.

Steamers of this type can accommodate silk up to one metre wide, although an extension tube can be fitted for widths of up to 1·5 metres. Depending on the make of steamer, between thirty and fifty metres of fabric can be steamed at one time.

As with the pressure-cooker method, the silk must be rolled in paper before steaming. Lay the silk out on the paper, making sure that the pieces do not overlap. Try to leave a margin of at least 5 cm at each side. Slowly and carefully roll the paper up, keeping the edges even. If you have used coloured or metallic guttas, wax, sugar, outliners or permanent markers, place another sheet or two of paper on top of the silk for added protection.

Continue to roll the paper for another metre and then seal the edge using tape. Seal each end of the tube with foil and tape. Lower the tube down into the cylinder on to the ring at the base. Secure the top ring and seal with the dome-shaped lid. Fill the base container with water and place the cylinder on top. Boil the water and steam for approximately three hours. The cylinder is double-walled, so that when the steam rises it condenses under the dome-shaped lid and then runs down between the walls to the base for re-use.

The same fixing paper can be used twice, providing it has no stains. If it is re-used, the fixing time must be prolonged by one hour, as the paper may have lost some of its

a

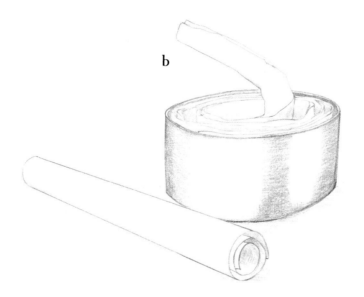

b

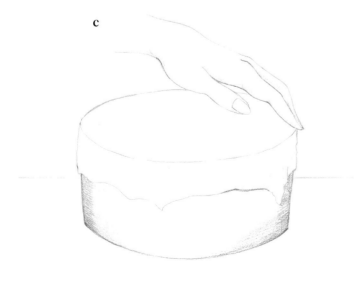

c

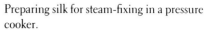

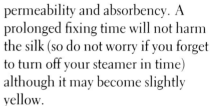

Preparing silk for steam-fixing in a pressure cooker.
(a) Roll silk in absorbent paper
(b) Coil roll into container
(c) Cover container with foil
(d) Silk steaming in a pressure cooker

permeability and absorbency. A prolonged fixing time will not harm the silk (so do not worry if you forget to turn off your steamer in time) although it may become slightly yellow.

Horizontal steamer
This is a long, stainless-steel box which can be heated on a gas or electric cooker. It can accommodate approximately eighteen metres of fabric up to 90 cm in width. Once again, make sure that no water penetrates the roll of paper and silk. Use the same method as for the vertical steamer. The water is held in the base of the vertical box and steaming takes 90 minutes.

The steaming process alters the colour of natural silk very slightly,

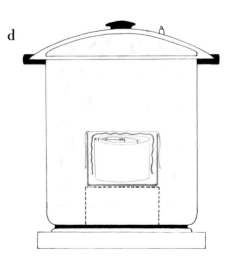

d

so if you are making a garment which includes an un-dyed piece of silk, remember to fix this at the same time.

Washing

After fixing (especially steam-fixing) you will notice that the colours on your silk have become more vibrant, and that the texture of the silk has a lustrous sheen. Rinse the silk thoroughly in warm water to remove any excess dye particles which may remain in the silk. You must always wash pieces separately, of course, as the colour may run a little. Reds and navy blues are more prone to running than other colours.

If the silk has been fixed correctly, the colour should remain just as bright after it has been washed. Large pieces of work need to be spread out to prevent marking just in case some excess dye does run, so a bath or large vessel is recommended.

After washing, lay the silk on a clean towel, roll it up gently and pat to remove excess moisture. We would suggest that the silk is ironed straight away, while still damp, as the creases will all be removed and a fine sheen will appear on the surface. Iron the silk with a steam iron, or an ordinary iron on a medium-hot setting. If you have used coloured or metallic gutta or outliners, be sure to iron on the reverse side of the silk.

Removal of gutta

If water-soluble gutta has been used, it will be removed at the washing stage. Solvent-based gutta can be left in the fabric, but will give the silk a soft, rubbery feel. Clear gutta can be removed by dry-cleaning or by immersing the silk in a large, screw-top jar of white spirit. Shake the jar thoroughly until all the gutta has dissolved. The silk must then be washed several times to get rid of the smell. When working with white spirit, open all your windows for ventilation, or work outside.

Dry-cleaning

If you are worried about washing the silk you can send it to be dry-cleaned, although this will not get rid of excess dye. *Do not* send silk to be dry-cleaned if you have used metallic or coloured gutta, glitter pens or outliners, as all of these would be removed, although there are now permanent guttas that will stay in the silk after dry-cleaning. Be sure to check on the gutta instructions, as so many different products are now available. If you are selling your hand-painted scarves and clothes, make sure that you put a 'DO NOT DRY-CLEAN' label on these items.

Your silk is now ready to be sewn or made into a wonderful, unique creation.

TIPS

- When steaming, make sure that you protect the silk adequately with paper, foil and tape.
- When steaming, do not place the silk too near the edges of the paper when rolling it up.
- Use two or three layers of fixing paper if coloured guttas, markers, outliners, wax or sugar have been used.
- To prevent too much creasing in the steamer, iron the silks before you roll them up in the paper.
- Metallic and coloured guttas often stick to the fixing paper and are hard to remove. To prevent this, unroll the fixings immediately while still hot, and very gently peel off the silk from the paper.

GLOSSARY

AIRBRUSH   A tool which sprays a fine film of colour; compressors or air-propellant cans also provide the pressurized air.

ANTIFUSANT   Also known as stop-flow or anti-spread, this is a liquid which controls the flow of the dyes on the surface of the silk and allows detailed work.

APPLIQUE   Pieces of fabric applied to a background fabric and held down with stitching.

BATIK   A technique involving the application of wax or starch to fabric in order to resist dye.

BLOCKPRINTING   Technique for hand-printing patterns on to cloth using a carved wooden or linoleum block.

CRACKING   Fine-line effects created with the wax technique.

DIFFUSER   A metal gadget used to spray dye on to silk by blowing through it.

DILUENT   Sometimes known as diffusant, diluant, anticerne or diffusion fondnet, this is a solution to help the even spreading of dyes.

DRESSING   A starch or glue-like substance added to fabric to stiffen it. It should be washed out before you start.

DYE BATH   A solution of dye and water in which silk is dyed.

ECO-SPRAY   Hand-held paint or dye spray. The fine jet of paint or dye is propelled by compressed air in a small canister.

EPAISSISANT   Also known as thickener, this can be mixed with dyes to form a paste-like substance which permits direct painting on to silk.

ESSENCE F   This is a solvent for gutta (solvent-based).

FASTNESS   A dye's ability to withstand washing, dry-cleaning and exposure to the light.

FIXING   The process by which colours are fixed permanently into the fabric.

GUTTA   A clear, coloured or metallic substance used to prevent silk paints from blending into each other. There are two types of gutta: solvent-based and water-based.

MASKING FLUID   A fluid which can be painted on to paper or fabric to mask or resist certain areas of the design from the dye. It may be rubbed off afterwards.

MONOPRINTING   Painting the dye on to a sheet of glass. A print can be taken by pressing silk on to the glass.

MOTIF   One unit of a pattern or design.

NOMOGRAPHIC NIB   A fine, metal-pointed nib with a hole through which the gutta is squeezed.

PIPETTE   A plastic dropper.

PROCION   Extremely strong dyes which do not require fixing after painting.

RESIST   A substance or material which prevents dye from reaching certain areas of the silk.

RUCHING   A method of gathering fabric into small folds.

SOLVENT   Liquid used to remove and dissolve.

STENCIL   Thin card with a design cut out.

TEXTURE   A surface quality.

THICKENER   *See* EPAISSISANT.

STOCKISTS, MANUFACTURERS AND SUPPLIERS

GREAT BRITAIN

Stockists

Edda Ashman
Les Guilberts
Route de la Palloterie
St Peters, Guernsey

(*Shop. Javana dyes and guttas. Silk and silk-painting equipment*)

Atlantis Paper Co. Ltd
2 St Andrews Way
London E3 3PA

(*Mail order. Sennelier dyes and silk-painting equipment*)

Candle Makers Suppliers
28 Blythe Road
London W14 0HA

(*Shop and mail order. Deka, Knaizeff and Pebeo dyes, silk-painting equipment and wax*)

Cornellissen and Sons Ltd
105 Great Russell Street
London WC1B 3RY

(*Shop and mail order. Sennelier and Elbesoie dyes and silk-painting equipment*)

Dryad Specialist Crafts Ltd
PO Box 247
Leicester LE1 9QS

(*Mail order. Kits, silk-painting equipment*)

Procion Dyes
Noel Dyrenforth
11 Shepherds Hill
London N6 5QJ

(*Mail order. Procion cold-water-reactive cantings and workshops*)

Suasion
35 Riding House Street
London W1P 7PT

Vycombe Arts Ltd
Fen Way
Fen Walk
Woodbridge
Suffolk IP12 4AS

(*Mail order. Pebeo and Deka dyes, silk and silk-painting equipment*)

George Weil
Old Portsmouth Road
Pease Marsh
Guildford
Surrey GU3 1LZ

(*Mail order. Javana, Deka, Dupont and Procion dyes. Speedball Hunt. Silk-painting equipment and fabrics*)

WS Touch Base
Wyevale Centre
Wareham Road
Owermigne
Dorchester
Dorset DT2 8BY

Manufacturers and suppliers

Colart UK Ltd
(Dryad, Reeves, Le Franc and Bourgeois)
Whitefriars Avenue
Harrow
Middlesex HA3 5RH

(*Elbesoie, Elbetex and Dryad kits*)

Dylon International
Worsley Bridge Road
Lower Sydenham
London SE26 5HD

(*Dylon dyes*)

Edding UK Ltd
Merlin Centre
Acrewood Way
St Albans
Herts AL4 0JY

(*Marabu dyes*)

H.W. Peel and Co.
1c Lyon Way
Rockware Estate
Greenford
Middlesex UB6 0BN

(*Sennelier dyes*)

I.C.I.
PO Box 42
Hexagon House
Blackley
Manchester M9 3DA

(*Procion dyes*)

Poth Hille and Co. Ltd
37 High Street
London E15 2QD
(*Wax manufacturers*)

Silk

MacCulloch and Wallis Ltd
25–6 Dering Street
London W1R 0BH

Pongées Ltd
184–6 Old Street
London EC1V 9PB

Pure Silk
Eddie Salter
Old Church Room
Hill Row
Haddenham
Cambridge CB6 37C

Whaleys (Bradford) Ltd
Harris Court
Bradford
West Yorkshire BD7 4EQ

CONTINENTAL EUROPE
Stockists

BELGIUM

La Fourmi
Rue Vanderkinder 236
1180 Brussels
(*Mail order and shop. Dupont, Deka, Pebeo and Ferfix dyes, silk and all silk-painting equipment*)

Passe-temps
Avenue Georges Henri 292
1200 Brussels
(*Shop. Dupont, Deka and Pebeo dyes, silk and all silk-painting equipment*)

FRANCE

L'Echeveau
11 Rue de la Monnaie
35000 Rennes
(*Dyes and all silk-painting equipment*)

Ponsard Freres
28 Rue du Sentier
75002 Paris
(*Mail order and shop. Kraizeff, Marabu and Pebeo dyes, silks and silk-painting equipment*)

GERMANY

Galerie Smend
Mainzer Strasse 31
Postfach 250360
5000 Koeln
(*Mail order and shop. Everything the silk painter could dream of, plus books and gallery*)

Verdener Bastel Studio
Postfach 1547–2810
Verden
(*Mail order. All silk-painting equipment*)

Manufacturers and suppliers

FRANCE

Dupont
Route de Guindreef
44600 Saint Nazaire
(*Dupont dyes and silk-painting equipment*)

Knaizeff
Ateliers Creative
18 Rue de Garet
6900 Lyon
(*Knaizeff dyes*)

Le Prince
19 Rue de Clery
75002 Paris
(*Princecolor, Princefix and silk-painting equipment*)

Pebeo
Usine St Marcel
13367 Marseille
(*Orient Express Pebeo Soie, Setacolor, Setaskrib and silk-painting equipment*)

Sennelier
Rue du Moulin à Cailloux
Orly, Senia 40894567
(*Super Tinfix, Peintex, Textecolor and silk*)

GERMANY

C. Kreul GmbH
Hainbrunnenstrasse 8
8550 Forchheim
(*Javana dyes*)

Deka
Kapellenstrasse 18
Munchen – Unterhaching
(*Deka dyes*)

Hobbidee und Frech Verlag (TOPP)
Turbinstrasse 7
7600 Stuttgart 31
(*Savoir Faire, Thermosilk and Dupont dyes, silk-painting equipment and TOPP books*)

Marabuwerke
7146 Tamm
(*Marabu textile and silk*)

Silkolor
B. Korbach Dipling
Postfach 1105
6501 Budenheim
(*Silkolor*)

Uhlig Horst Uhlig
Horst Uhlig Strasse
8449 Laudert
(*Steamers, dyes and silk-painting equipment*)

HOLLAND

Toba
Voortsweg 99
7523CD Enschede
(*Tobasign dyes*)

USA

Stockists

Art Supply Warehouse
360 Main Avenue Route 7
Norwalk
Connecticut 06851

(*Mail order. Deka dyes, silks and silk-painting equipment*)

Dharma Trading Co.
PO Box 150916
San Rafael
California 94915

(*Mail order. Procion, Deka, Versatex, Sennelier, Pebeo and Jacquard dyes. Everything the silk painter needs. Fabrics, steamers and clothes made ready-to-paint*)

Fabdec
3553 Old Post Road
San Angelo
Texas 76904

(*Mail order. Procion dyes and fabrics*)

Sureway Trading Enterprises
826 Pine Avenue
Suite 506
Niagara Falls
New York 14301

(*Mail order. Silks, Sennelier dyes and silk-painting equipment*)

Silk

Oriental Silk Co.
8377 Beverley Boulevard
Los Angeles
California 90048

(*Mail order. Silks*)

AUSTRALIA

Stockist

Oetoro Pty Ltd
PO Box 324
Coogee
NSW 2034

(*Mail order. Dyes and silk-painting equipment, fabrics and books*)

We would like to thank the following companies, which provided some of the materials used in our samples: Cornellissen and Sons Ltd, Atlantis Paper Co. Ltd, Colart UK Ltd, Edding UK Ltd, Galerie Smend, Le Prince, Dupont, Sennelier, Toba, Hobbidee und Frech Verlag (TOPP), Deka, Ivy Imports and Cerulean Blue Ltd.

USEFUL ADDRESSES

STEAMING SERVICES

If you do not have access to a steaming machine and would like to use transparent steam-fixed dyes, the following run steaming services:

Candle Makers Suppliers
28 Blythe Road
London W14 0HA

Vycombe Arts Ltd
Fen way
Fen walk
Woodbridge
Suffolk IP12 9AS

SEWING SERVICES

Ties, buttons, ear-rings, belts, bow-ties, cravats, clutch bags, bows, evening bags and hair accessories

Harlequin
E.A and H. M Bull Ltd
Lawford
Manningtree
Essex CO11 1UX

Card mounts

Craft Creations
Units 1–7
Harpers Yard
Ruskin Road
Tottenham
London N17 8NE

Impress
Slough Farm
Westhall
Halesworth
Suffolk IP19 8RN

INDEX